A Different View of Urban Schools

"Some U.S. policy makers were so disturbed by the power of the civil rights movement that they have been revising the story ever since, implying that African American leadership did not accomplish much of substance, especially in the field of education. In this book, Kitty Kelly Epstein presents a clear record of African American achievement in challenging inequity, even in an arena as filled with confusion as the world of American public schools."

Danny Glover, Actor, Producer, and Social Activist

"Kitty Kelly Epstein tells a fascinating revisionist history of the evolution and struggles around public education. She is uniquely qualified to do so since she is a central participant in urban school events and a theorist on American education. Epstein joins the short list of social scientists who have studied their problem by embedding themselves in it personally. The result provides a new perspective on what educational reform requires in American cities."

John Roemer, Elizabeth S. and A. Varick Stout Professor
of Political Science and Economics,
Department of Political Science, Yale University

"Kitty Kelly Epstein is a bold and visionary activist, educator, and storyteller. In this clear account, she analyzes a history of racism in education politics in order to argue for a living, active, and inclusive democracy. She shows us convincingly that, only by being honest about racism in our past and present, can we construct the excellent schools that urban communities want and deserve."

Christine Sleeter, Emeritus Professor,
California State University Monterey Bay;
Author of Multicultural Education as Social Activism

D0888857

"Parents, teachers, and social activists should read *A Different View of Urban Schools*. It describes the little-known racial roots of standardized testing; the challenge the northern civil rights movement presented to institutionalized racism in American education; the success of this ongoing movement in challenging the tracking system, racist textbooks, and the lack of teachers of color; and the undemocratic maneuvers of conservative sectors of the white business community who were intent on returning urban school districts to their control."

Hari Dillon, President, Vanguard Public Foundation

"Kitty Kelly Epstein's scholarship is embedded in her lifetime of active engagement in the educational civil rights struggle. She deconstructs, chapter and verse, the many 'urban myths' about public schools held by both liberals and conservatives and posits an alternate argument based on 'five, basic, unchanging and generally unmentioned realities' about U.S. education. . . .

Epstein's book is imbued with a 'critical hope' based on her existential understanding that without struggles at both the school and societal levels, there is no educational progress. She argues persuasively that rigorous critique and struggles within schools, school systems, and the society at large can provide the momentum for transformative educational and social change.' Having chronicled the past successes of such progressive struggles in Oakland, she outlines the makings of a multiracial, 'people's program for educational change.' Her book is a clear-noted reveille for the necessary national movement for education as a civil right."

Luis O. Reyes, Visiting Fellow, Lehman College, CUNY;
Former Member, New York City Board of Education

A Different View of
Urban Schools

Studies in the
Postmodern Theory of Education

Joe L. Kincheloe and Shirley R. Steinberg
General Editors

Vol. 291

PETER LANG
New York • Washington, D.C./Baltimore • Bern
Frankfurt am Main • Berlin • Brussels • Vienna • Oxford

Kitty Kelly Epstein

A Different View of Urban Schools

Civil Rights, Critical Race Theory, and Unexplored Realities

PETER LANG
New York • Washington, D.C./Baltimore • Bern
Frankfurt am Main • Berlin • Brussels • Vienna • Oxford

Library of Congress Cataloging-in-Publication Data

Epstein, Kitty Kelly.
A different view of urban schools: civil rights, critical race theory,
and unexplored realities / Kitty Kelly Epstein.
p. cm.— (Counterpoints: studies in the postmodern theory of education; v. 291)
Includes bibliographical references and index.
1. Urban schools—United States. 2. Racism in education—United States.
3. Educational equalization—United States.
I. Title. II. Series: Counterpoints (New York, N.Y.); v. 291.
LC5141.E67   370'.9173'2—dc22   2005022532
ISBN 978-0-8204-7879-1
ISSN 1058-1634

Bibliographic information published by **Die Deutsche Bibliothek**.
Die Deutsche Bibliothek lists this publication in the "Deutsche
Nationalbibliografie"; detailed bibliographic data is available
on the Internet at http://dnb.ddb.de/.

Cover design by Joni Holst
Top cover photo of McClymond High School's 2005 graduates:
Nishay Stewart, Candase Chambers, Delvan Napier, Monica Foster,
Ashley Hirsch, Burt Jones, Violet Jennings, Frank Brogan, Patreka Adam, and Kevin Battle
(Photo by Zusha Elinson, used by permission from the Post Newspaper Group)

The paper in this book meets the guidelines for permanence and durability
of the Committee on Production Guidelines for Book Longevity
of the Council of Library Resources.

To my son, Jaron,
a deep and thoughtful person
with a passion for social justice.

CONTENTS

Acknowledgments

I MOST APPRECIATE THE UNNAMED THOU-
sands who have struggled for a hundred and forty years
to create justice and enlightenment in urban school dis-
tricts across this country. In the modern era this includes
some personal friends: Keith Brown, Alona Clifton, Gay
Cobb, Paul Cobb, Audrey Cuff, Hari Dillon, Jim and
Arley Dann, Mildred Edordu, Fred Ellis, Ken Epstein,
Selehi Garrett, Danny Glover, Lenneal Henderson, Liz
Henry, Mekael Johnson, Joyce Germaine Watts, Henry Hitz, Harold Berlak, Pat Williams Myrick, Geoffrey
Pete, Luis Reyes, Walter Riley, John and Natasha Roemer,
Linda Segundo, Faye Stallings, Peggy and Bob Stinnett,
Lorna Jones, Bernard Stringer, Susan Taira, Paul Takagi,
and Joyce Germaine Watts. My deep respect to The Van-
guard Foundation, the Structural Inequality and Diversity
Task Force, and Rob McKay for providing the community
atmosphere, the dialogue, and the resources necessary to

work on issues of peace, justice, and democracy. Hugs to several thousand high school students, college students, prospective teachers, and graduate students who have provided endless pleasure and stimulation while I muddled through this analysis.

Deepest love to my parents, Andrew and Edna Kelly, for giving me life, to my sister Robin, and to other family and friends, including Jaron Kelly Epstein, Betsy Shultz, Ken Toth, Ken Toth, Jr., Danrey Toth, Emma Toth, Debbie Wyatt, Kenny and Christina Wyatt, Barbara Avery, Karen Teel, Kim Mayfield, Dakiem Anderson Ellis, Roz Wolf, Dennis Gregg, Roberta Frye, and Pat Margulies, who have given many hugs and much support over the years

My thanks to Christine Sleeter for helping me think that someone might publish this book and to Gloria Ladson-Billings for being a role model to all academics who care about social justice.

1

Themes and Theories, Personal and Academic

I NEVER REALLY DECIDED TO TEACH. I WAS propelled into it by the barely moving clock hanging above my desk at the collection agency where I addressed threatening notices to tardy customers. I was finishing college and had not considered occupations very much. I took credential classes to escape the deadening routine of the office, and in the process I found teaching to be a job so thrilling that I would have done it even if no one were paying me. Everything about teaching was exciting—the ideas, the sociability, the opportunity to plan events for thirty young human beings. And eventually teaching led me back to confronting the sort of large and small civil rights issues which had filled my student years.

I have looked at schools from a dozen different angles. I have substituted at every grade level and have taught high school in Oakland, community college in Hayward, and

undergraduates at U.C. Berkeley. I have prepared teachers, masters' candidates, and doctoral students. And I have
been an active parent. I have investigated schools from
the front of the classroom, as a teacher, and from the back
of the classroom, as a parent. I have investigated from a
scholar's vantage point in libraries and archives, and from
a participant researcher's spot in community gatherings,
union meetings, and boardrooms. In the process I have
concluded that schools in this period are a preeminent
place of social struggle in the U.S. Many Americans have
abandoned even the hope of fairness in the marketplace,
the bureaucracy, and the health care system. But they still
expect schools to be fair, to provide opportunity, justice,
skills, and enlightenment. And when the schools are not
fair and nurturing, people are willing to struggle about the
ideas and issues which undergird this failure.

By living the events in one school district and studying
the events in others, I have concluded that the actual operation of urban schools is obscured by a number of myths
and false debates. The story line of the most important
myth goes like this: Urban schools brought enlightenment
and basic education to masses of Americans from the early
part of the 20ᵗʰ century to the 1960s. Then these schools
became chaotic, violent, corrupt, and dysfunctional, and,
as a result, responsible people, including those in state
and federal governments, academics, and businesses, have
been forced to intervene to save the children attending
these schools. The new federal education law, commonly
called "No Child Left Behind," is based on this premise.
The state takeover of school districts which has occurred
in Detroit, Philadelphia, Compton, Oakland, and many
other districts is based on the same reasoning.

Many liberals have rejected No Child Left Behind on
the basis that its accountability measures are flawed, that its
mandates are unfunded, and that it will lead to the priva-

tization of public education. However, these critics do not generally reject the underlying faulty historical logic, and so their reasoning is hard to sustain: If the schools are screwed up and the people currently in charge of them are responsible for the mess, why shouldn't somebody else take over?

In this book I will present an alternate argument to that accepted by both liberals and conservatives. The elements of this alternate argument are the following: 1) public schools, especially urban schools, were not good before the 1960s, at least not for the Latino, African American, and Asian students who attended them; 2) intense but little known civil rights battles took place in many Northern cities; 3) The post-1960s school boards which resulted from these struggles did not "screw up" the schools but, within existing constraints, made progress on equity issues; 4) These equity policies have produced some advances in civil rights and cultural sensitivity; 5) urban school districts were increasingly constrained by state and federal policies and then direct intervention; 6) the logic, structures, and practices of American racism flow throughout both the history and the current period.

In addition to the "schools were o.k. in the good old days" myth, a second and related myth concerns the relationship between "learning" and all other aspects of school. Both liberals and conservatives focus their rhetoric on the classroom aspect: Is there morality? Is the reading method effective? Both liberals and conservatives argue that we should "forget adult agendas" and "focus on classroom achievement," as though the recent urban school boards have been unusually and unethically worried about economics and power. The school events in which I participated have led me to conclude that while well-meaning people are "ignoring the politics" and "focusing on the classroom," they are losing the political and economic battles, so that neither educational nor economic and political justice is possible.

WHO NEEDS A THEORY?

Without a theoretical framework, those concerned with schools toss around an endless set of piecemeal arguments. We engage in debates about phonics versus whole language instruction. Public schools vs. charters. Vouchers vs. no vouchers. Graduation exams or no exams. Segregation or integration. And a thousand other debates which come and go with the latest think tank or newspaper report.

Important as these individual debates may be, there are five basic, unchanging, and generally unmentioned realities about U.S. education, realities which impact every other debate.

1. The U.S. is a capitalist country. Money speaks, and disguised battles over who gets the money often have far more influence than pedagogical concerns in many educational decisions.

2. The entire U.S. education system sits on a structure of tests and sorting invented by members of the Eugenics movement who believed Northern European whites to be smarter than everyone else. Thus, every aspect of U.S. education, from the selection of teachers to the assessment of students, has race as an essential, if unacknowledged, component.

3. Democracy is limited. The more white and affluent the parents of a particular group of children, the more likely they will have real influence over expenditures, curriculum, nurturance, school structure, and personnel selection. When districts with less affluent citizens make different decisions about these issues, their power to make the decisions is increasingly circumscribed.

4. There is no single public. When politicians discuss what "we" should do about American schools they are advanc-

ing a "harmful fiction." (Ladson-Billings & Tate, 1995) There are actually four different American systems: the somewhat responsive suburban and middle class public system; the urban systems, many of which have been taken over by outside state, federal, or private interests; the system of private and parochial schools for working class and urban children which are not well-funded but are still somewhat responsive to their local communities; and the system of elite private schools to which the wealthy send their own children but which are required to follow none of the rules and procedures which have been established to control the schools attended by the poor.

5. Nevertheless, Americans students, parents, labor unions, civil rights groups, and community groups have on many occasions successfully challenged the structures and policies which result from the first four realities.

THEORETICAL COMPONENTS

The theoretical framework of this book draws from the following sources:

1. Critical race theory, which emphasizes the elements of racism deeply embedded within every institution and event in American society;

2. Marxist method, not as a set of conclusions, but as a process of investigation which is historical, dialectical, and materialist, and looks at individual phenomenon from within the totality of all phenomenon; and

3. The thinking of such recent activists as Paulo Freire, who talks about the international phenomenon of schools as "sites of struggle."

These theoretical elements are woven throughout the analysis and will be briefly defined in this first chapter.

CRITICAL RACE THEORY

Critical race theory emerged within the field of law and began to be used by educators with the publication of an essay by Gloria Ladson-Billings and William Tate in 1995. Among the important contributions of this theory are the following contentions: 1) race is undertheorized as an aspect of U.S. society and education; 2) racism is rooted in property relations; and 3) racism is permanent in U.S. society (Ladson-Billings & Tate, 1995; Bell, 2004). Attention to each of these can remove some blinders as we look at urban schools, blinders imposed by the very pervasive nature of U.S. racism. As we ask, for example, why is there an "achievement gap" between black and white students, these three contentions can help us look more clearly. First, we will be more likely to look for racial structures, rather than individual student characteristics, to explain the gap. Second, we will understand that it may be connected to issues of property, particularly "whiteness" as a possession in and of itself. And third, we will not be expecting an easy fix through some new government policy.

MARXISM

Why bring up Marx, the reader may wonder? He is seen as such a villain that we might be better off just using the general approaches described earlier without attributing them to any particular person. He is not the only thinker to use history or dialectics, and anyway, he's not alive to complain if we ignore him. But accepting the villain image for those who challenge injustice deprives us of the transformative possibilities in their insights and histories. This applies to

Marx as surely as it does to those civil rights leaders who made the contributions described in this book.

I will not attempt to discuss Marx's specific economic or political conclusions. Whatever one's views on these issues, elements of the method used by Marx can lead to a deeper and broader understanding of the place of urban schools in U.S. society. Marx placed everything in historical context (Wallis, 1998). Because we use little history in American educational debates, we recycle old problems and old solutions. Reformers would be less baffled by the bureaucratic, impersonal nature of U.S. high schools, for example, if they examined the ways in which these qualities were purposely structured into the schools by their creators (Tyack, 1974). Marx used dialectical thinking and saw social development taking place as a result of contradictions between various forces and interests. He saw the seeds of the future in the structures of the present, and of particular importance for those in education, thought that late-stage capitalism would develop more and more forms of education and training, because of technical innovation and job differentiation. Recognizing this dialectical process of change is important for those in education, because it is different from the frequently expressed idea that changes in education occur as a cycle or a pendulum, returning always to the same point. Marx was also a materialist who analyzed the economic underpinnings of phenomenon (Elliott, 1987). And he considered each phenomenon within the context of other phenomenon. That is, he did not look at health or education or jobs or advertising in isolation. Again, our modern critical analysis of education is often missing this quality. We engage in debates on the best curriculum or the best school structure without regard to the impact which business or political influence is certain to have on these debates.

FREIRIANS—SCHOOLS AS SITES OF STRUGGLE

Paulo Freire made an international contribution to humane and antielitist pedagogy. Within the context of this book his most important contribution has to do with the mind-set of individuals within school systems which appear to be both unfair and hegemonic. If the logic of critical race theory and Marxist analysis lead us to understand the educational system as embedded within a broader system of political and economic power, we are likely to conclude that neither policy changes nor better teaching will rectify the inequality. And here Freire's notion of schools as places where people struggle for justice with "critical hope" (as opposed to utopian hope) is an important contribution (Freire, 1994).

This book utilizes all of these approaches and insights when examining urban schools. We begin with a revisionist history, noting the often-ignored racial dynamics of Northern cities. We proceed with the struggles and contradictions, particularly over the expenditure of money, which occurred when African Americans finally had enough political clout to make decisions about urban schools. And then we look at the generally ignored accomplishments of these more representative school boards, noting as Freire does that schools are sites of struggle and sometimes those struggles are successful.

THE LOCATION OF THE STUDY AND THE CHARACTERISTICS OF THE RESEARCHER

In this book I will elaborate upon the operation of the five realities mentioned above in one notorious urban school system. I have chosen Oakland for several reasons: 1) I am here, imbedded in the ways I have described above. I know it infinitely better than most academics know the systems they study. 2) Oakland exists within one of the most "progressive" constituencies in America. Oakland's Congress-woman Lee was the only congressional vote against the war in Iraq, for example, and after that vote she was re-elected by a margin of 85 percent to 15 percent. And yet, as the book will demonstrate, Oakland's "progressives" have acted in ways which often divide rather than unify. 3) although Oakland is not the largest urban district, it is one of the most famous, reaching the headlines of the *New York Times* and CBS on many occasions with issues such as Ebonics and textbook selection. Thus, even a distant international audience has found Oakland's ferocious battles over the nature and structure of urban education to be noteworthy.

I have already identified my multifaceted relationship to the subject of my study. I do not believe that any social science research is neutral. Thus, I consider the depth of my knowledge to be a benefit rather than a curse, but the reader will have to judge for herself. As a white woman, I recognize that the story I tell is influenced by my own race and class position. Though I am deeply concerned with civil rights, my perspective is not and could not be the perspective of a Latino or Asian or African American woman. Again, there are advantages and disadvantages. I may suffer fewer repercussions than a person of color in speaking frankly about race; on the other hand my perception of these issues is certain to be less sharp in some ways than the perspective of one who experiences, as a victim, the racial attitudes and policies I am describing.

Oakland, California, is a large city with a student population that is 93 percent African African, Latino, Asian, and Native American, and it is a district to which the mythology described earlier is frequently applied. The main evidence offered for this outlook is the low test scores of city children. However, since family wealth remains the best predictor of test scores in every school district, the scores simply indicate the extent to which more affluent children were leaving the Oakland schools while poor children were joining them.

In this book I show that the Oakland schools were *not* effective 50 years ago, especially not for the Latino and African American students who attended them. For many years the city government and school board were dominated by a conservative political machine that was unresponsive to requests from immigrant and African American communities. Then, beginning in the late 1960s, a sophisticated, broad-based educational civil rights movement brought non-white school boards to power. These boards did not "mess up the schools," but initiated important new policies that have helped to move the country forward in educational equity. Oakland's movement won victories in minority hiring and contracting, stopped a state takeover, and rejected racially insensitive textbooks. They did not succeed in transforming all the schools into the personal, peaceful, and rigorous learning environments that both they and Oakland parents would desire. However, I argue that this was not within their power, and that their critics at the state and federal level bear the largest burden of responsibility for what is not effective in Oakland and other urban districts.

A note on vocabulary: All of the words which group Latino, African American, Asian, and Native American people together—"minority," "non-white," "people of color"—are problematic because they define people in relation to whiteness. In some places I list the groups being discussed individually. In other places I use the problematic terms because I have not found a better solution, not because I think they fairly represent the world.

A note on what's missing: There are many vital education issues which are unexplored or partially explored in this book. Among these are 1) teachers unions, which are some of the most progressive national unions on social policy issues; 2) depth and detail about pedagogy, particularly at the high school level; 3) an exploration of the agenda of organizations like the Business Roundtable; 4) differences between liberal and right-wing capitalists in their approach to restructuring the educational system; 5) the initiative of organizations affiliated with the "Algebra Project" to have education recognized as a civil right. I have much to say on each of these topics, but that must be left to other books. In the meantime, I urge readers to check out the Web sites of the mentioned organizations and the pedagogical work of Gloria Ladson-Billings.

2

The Bad Old Days

The Pre–Civil Rights History of a Northern School District

AN UNSTATED ASSUMPTION IN MOST DIS-
cussions of urban school district reform is the notion that
these districts have declined in the last quarter century
and are providing less adequate education than in a pre-
vious era. In this chapter I look closely at that assumption. Drawing on information from personal interviews as
well as from archival data, I examine the use of Oakland as
the first laboratory to employ IQ testing for "tracking" an
entire school district, the racial climate that flourished in
Oakland, starkly evidenced by widespread Ku Klux Klan
activity, the individual experiences of students and teachers of color in these early years, and the quality of facilities, governance opportunities, and classroom experience
for people of color during that period.

OBSCURING RACE IN MAKING POLICY

Mayor Jerry Brown, speaking to a city council meeting on November 30, 1999, declared, "The Oakland schools have been going bad for twenty years." Based on this assessment, Brown supported removal of the power of the local board. Brown neglected to note that his twenty-year benchmark, 1979, was one of the first years when African Americans had significant influence on the school board.

Proposals to remove local control were never made during the eighty years when the district was led entirely by white school boards and superintendents, although, as we shall see, there were accusations of corruption, and conditions for students were not good. Brown's treatment of this issue illustrates an important feature of critical race theory: the failure of policy makers to discuss race in the making of policies which have profoundly racial consequences.

RACIAL MYTHOLOGIES

Oakland's "celebrity Mayor" Jerry Brown is not the first person to imply that Black governance had "messed up" otherwise happy, well-run parts of America. Historian James Loewen reports on a class he taught on Southern history in which students came to similar conclusions.

"I was about to launch into a unit on Reconstruction, and I needed to find out what the students already knew... The class consensus: Reconstruction was the time when African-Americans took over the governing of the Southern states, including Mississippi. But they were too soon out of slavery, so they messed up and reigned corruptly, and whites had to take back control of the state governments."

"I sat stunned," Loewen continues. "So many major misconceptions glared from that statement that it was hard to know where to begin a rebuttal." (Loewen, 1996, p. 156)

Loewen was especially pained because this class took place at Tougaloo College, a predominantly black school in Mississippi. Black students were victimized by a racist mythology about their own history! In fact African Americans did not "mess up." Mississippi had less corrupt government during Reconstruction than in the following decades. White Democrats used force to wrest control from the multiracial Reconstruction coalitions which emerged in Mississippi after the Civil War, and thereafter Mississippi suffered from decades of ruthless discrimination and stagnation.

OAKLAND'S MYTHS

The myths believed by Loewen's students are echoed in similar myths about Oakland. Specifically I will argue that 1) powerful white businessmen and politicians held most of the real power in the Oakland schools for the entire 20th century; 2) as people of color began to hold positions as school board members and administrators, they tried to remedy some injustices; 3) such modern school issues as low test scores and low expectations had their origins in early 20th century Oakland, where the first standardized tests were tried out as a mechanism for tracking the entire school system.

(A note on the information in this chapter: Data on African Americans are more accessible, during the early history, than data on Latinos or Asians. The census, for example, does not list Latinos as a separate category until after 1930.)

OAKLAND'S OLD BOYS

The very names attached to the Oakland school district administration building tell a story about the struggle over racial justice. During the 1990s, the building itself, at 1025 2nd Avenue, was named the Paul Robeson Building, in honor of Shakespearean actor, opera singer, football player, Rhodes scholar, and blacklisted activist Paul Robeson, who visited Oakland in the 1940s to support a general strike. But upstairs in the same building there is a cavernous fourth-floor auditorium in which teachers are in-serviced and to which overflowing school board crowds are directed. This auditorium, Hunter Hall, still bears the name of a man few Oaklanders recognize, Superintendent Fred Hunter, who brought race-based tracking to the Oakland schools during the 1920s.

Fred Hunter did not believe that women should vote. He was so adamant about this that as superintendent of the Oakland schools he paid to have antisuffrage politicians address a mandatory teachers' meeting. He did not like unions either, and as president of the National Education Association he led a convention audience in booing a representative of the striking Kansas mine workers in 1921.

Upton Sinclair was the famous muckraking author of *The Jungle*, the exposé which is credited with creating the laws that regulate the meatpacking industry. Sinclair wrote another book, *The Goslings*, in which he undertook a similar exposé of American education, demonstrating in detail the extent to which educational decisions were made for profit-based reasons. Sinclair says Oakland's Hunter was a pawn for business: "The City of Oakland voted five million dollars for new schools; and Mr. Hunter explained publicly his idea that the proper people to handle these bonds were the businessmen; therefore he appointed a special committee known as the 'Bond Expenditure Committee.' This committee proceeded to appoint a prominent politician as 'land agent' to handle the buying of sites, at a salary of three hundred dollars a month. The opposition members of the school board objected to this program, and forced the resignation of the Bond Expenditure committee: whereupon, Mr. Hunter caused to be printed in the Oakland 'Tribune,' kept newspaper of the gang, an interview proclaiming to the citizens that the school system was about to be disrupted." (Sinclair, 1924)

Superintendent Hunter also participated in graft, according to Upton Sinclair. In fact, when the old school board insisted that the contractors live up to their agreements in the building of new schools, Hunter campaigned against the board members and had them replaced by a more pliable board. "The first action of Mr. Hunter when the new board came in was to recommend the discharge and force the resignation of the too honest chief of construction." (Sinclair, 1924)

OAKLAND: A LABORATORY FOR SCIENTIFIC RACISM

Hunter's most important role, however, may have been as the superintendent who turned the Oakland school district into a laboratory for the pervasive use of IQ testing and tracking.

IQ tests were created by academics who believed that Northern European whites were smarter than everyone else and that this could be demonstrated by the tests they were developing.

Stanford professor and IQ test developer Lewis Terman explained his views in his textbook, *The Measurement of Intelligence* (1916), a book which was used in teacher education classes for decades following its first publication:

> Among laboring men and servant girls there are thousands like them (feebleminded individuals). They are the world's 'hewers of wood and drawers of water.' And yet, as far as intelligence is concerned, the tests have told the truth...No amount of school instruction will ever make them intelligent voters or capable voters in the true sense of the word....The fact that one meets this type with such frequency among Indians, Mexicans, and Negroes sug-

gests quite forcibly that the whole question of racial differences in mental traits will have to be taken up anew and by experimental methods. (Terman, pp. 91–92)

Terman became interested in the study of intelligence when a book peddler and phrenologist visited his family farm. The peddler predicted good things for Terman after feeling the bumps on his skull!

Terman became a professor at Stanford, and in 1916 he revised the test developed by France's Stephen Binet. He began calling it the "Stanford-Binet," and the test became the standard for virtually all IQ tests.

AN EXAMPLE FROM TERMAN'S TEST

Famed biologist Stephen J. Gould in his scathing critique of the concept of IQ provides one example from Terman's tests to illustrate the extent to which these tests stressed conformity with expectation and downgraded original responses.

"An Indian who had come to town for the first time in his life saw a white man riding along the street. As the white man rode by, the Indian said—'The white man is lazy; he walks sitting down.' What was the white man riding on that caused the Indian to say, 'He walks sitting down.'

"Terman accepted 'bicycle' as the only correct response. Car, horse, 'a cripple in a wheel chair' and 'a person riding on someone's back' were all marked wrong." (Gould, 1996, p. 177)

OAKLAND AS THE PERFECT LABORATORY

Oakland was rapidly growing, diverse, and mostly working class at the time Terman was developing his test in nearby Palo Alto. Moore Shipbuilding, Durant Motor Company,

Shredded Wheat, and Union Iron Works were just a few of the Oakland companies employing tens of thousands of those called "hewers of wood and drawers of water" by Terman (Bagwell, 1982, p. 190).

Ten percent of Oaklanders were African American or Asian and they were treated to disrespect and segregation. For example, a leaflet put out by the Laymance Real Estate Company in 1911 said, "It is probably unnecessary even to mention that no one of African or Mongolian descent will ever be allowed to own a lot in Rockridge or even rent any house that may be built there" (Bagwell, 1982, p. 206).

The Oakland schools had grown from 12,000 students in 1900 to over 48,000 students in 1918 (this includes an annexation which took place between 1900 and 1918) (Report of the Superintendent, 1917–18).

Oakland was exactly the sort of city Terman's colleague, Professor Elwood Cubberly, was describing when he said in 1909, "Our city schools will soon be forced to give up the exceedingly democratic idea that all are equal and our society devoid of classes...and to begin a specialization of educational effort along many lines in an attempt to adapt the school to the needs of these many classes." (Cubberly, 1916, p. 338)

In addition, Oakland was only thirty miles from Stanford and Oakland's Director of Research under Fred Hunter was Virgil Dickson, a student of Lewis Terman. Dickson and Terman began an extensive experiment on the use of IQ tests for the purpose of specializing or tracking students' educational careers. Dickson intended to demonstrate that students who were failing in school were stupid rather than poorly educated.

In a general report by the city superintendent of schools, dated June 1917, children were classified as normal, backward, borderline, moron, imbecile and idiot, or moral imbecile. Of 1,700 children tested, only 10 percent were classified as normal. Forty-one percent were classified borderline, and 23 percent were labeled moron. The report states that "the solution of the training of the mental defectives is one of the most important problems to confront the Board of Education. It is not just to these nor to normal children to attempt to train them together in graded classes . . . I wish to renew the recommendation I made a year ago that . . . this department be placed under the general supervision of Dr. Lewis Terman of Stanford University, a recognized expert on the diagnosis and training of mental defectives."

In an October 1925 superintendent's bulletin focusing on the Oakland junior high schools, vocational education is heralded for some populations as "the difference between a trend toward good citizenship . . . or a trend toward crime." IQ testing is described as the chief means for determining appropriate schooling for students. The report states that "the development of a scientific system of mental testing has given the teacher and school administrator a new instrument for the adaptation of school organization and methods to pupil needs."

Terman explained that "mental tests given to nearly 30,000 children in Oakland prove conclusively that the proportion of failures due chiefly to mental inferiority is nearer 90 percent than 50 percent." (Tyack, 1974, p. 209) He considered the obvious solution to be tracking, and constructed five tracks from "accelerated" to "atypical."

While the superintendent's report asserted that teachers and principals were overjoyed with these developments, a Berkeley graduate student and Oakland teacher, Ida Jackson, says otherwise. "In many schools the Principal and many of the teachers do not believe in the validity of the intelligence tests." (Jackson, 1923)

Oakland was not the only city to use IQ testing and ability grouping. In 1925, 215 cities used intelligence tests.

Of 40 cities with a population of at least 100,000, 37 used ability grouping in 1926. Secondary schools used the tests to organize ability grouping and also to guide the choice of careers (Tyack, 1974, p. 208).

KLANSMEN—IN OAKLAND??

What was the political atmosphere of a city which became the first location for such an experiment?

Oakland was, first of all, a booming city. Its population had grown from 66,960 in 1900 to 216,261 by 1920. It had absorbed refugees from the 1906 San Francisco earthquake, annexed the township of Brooklyn (now East Oakland), and attracted employees to work for Southern Pacific in the West Coast terminus of three transcontinental rail lines. Whites of "foreign stock" were 61 percent of the population in 1910, but the "native white" population was growing—from 39 to 44 percent of all whites between 1910 and 1920.

Much of Oakland politics was governed by people associated with Mike Kelly, a Catholic who served as Alameda County treasurer and later county tax collector. He was opposed by "good government" organizations like the Alameda County Organization, which put out a leaflet in 1918 accusing the Kelly alliance of "obtaining support from liquor interests and gambling joints." Opposition to Kelly was enhanced by Protestant middle-class prejudice against poor people and Catholics and sentiment in favor of prohibition. The political factions associated with Mike Kelly tended to be located in the older areas of West Oakland; the middle-class organizing tended to be located in the newer sections of recently incorporated East Oakland (Rhomberg, 1998).

During the decade of the 20s, civic politics of white native-born middle-class Oaklanders provided a fertile ground for the development of a white "nativist" and racist movement.

In August 1921, the Knights of the Ku Klux Klan, Inc. opened an office in downtown Oakland. On May 5, 1922, fifteen hundred men in white robes and masks gathered in the Oakland hills to burn a fiery cross behind an American flag in an initiation ceremony for five hundred new Ku Klux Klan recruits. In the six years from 1922 to 1927 the Klan amassed sufficient political power to conduct ceremonies for eighty-five hundred at the Oakland Auditorium and to elect several public officials, including the Piedmont chief of police, Burton F. Becker. William H. Parker was vice-president of Klan No. 9. He was a realtor and insurance salesman, active in the Dimond Progressive Club and first president of the East Oakland Consolidated Clubs, an association of thirty neighborhood improvement clubs.

In the 1923 election Grand Cyclops Leon Francis won 18 percent of the vote in a crowded field of school board candidates.

Contrary to traditional interpretations of 1920s Klan activity, it is not the case that the Klansmen represented marginal groups. Oakland Klansmen included Protestant churchmen, members of the Oakland fire department, the son of a congressman, professionals, and small businessmen.

In 1930 then district attorney Earl Warren began pursuing a case against Klansman Sheriff Becker. Says researcher Chris Rhomberg, "Even at this time, Klan legitimacy in Oakland was high enough that Warren feared that Klan members on the Alameda County Grand Jury would refuse to indict fellow Klansmen." (1998, p. 5)

Although Warren did successfully prosecute Becker and several other Klansmen, Rhomberg continues, "The defeat of the Klan, however, did not necessarily hinder the agenda of white middle-class Protestants as a group. The latter transferred their allegiance from the faulty vehicle of the Klan to the more effective anti-machine reformers among the business elite." (1998, p. 5)

1960: AN ELITE SCHOOL BUILT FOR OAKLAND'S AFFLUENT NEWCOMERS

Oakland was ruled by a "conservative Republican white male oligarchy for generations." (Snapp, 1999, p.8) During the 1950s affluent whites built more houses in the Oakland hills. In 1960 a whole school was built to track the hills students away from the non-white population of the flatlands. Before Skyline High was built, the high school zones of Oakland were drawn roughly from hilltop to bay. But the new school boundaries drawn for Skyline marked the entire hills region, from the Caldecott Tunnel to the San Leandro border, as the Skyline High School zone.

UNEQUAL CONDITIONS IN THE EARLY 1900s

TRACKING

The results of the tracking system can be discerned from those who lived under it.

Lifetime Oakland resident and educator, C.T. recalls her conversation with a counselor at Oakland Technical High School in 1967. When she inquired about college, the counselor told her, "Oh, I don't think that's for you. You need a vocational school." C.T. informed the counselor that her mother already had plans for her to attend college. After this experience, C.T. was leery of all counselors and made some costly mistakes in college as a result.

R.F., also a native Oaklander, recalls another form of tracking practiced against Chicano high school students during this period. With the beginning of the Vietnam War, counselors at her high school, Fremont, advised male

Latinos, even those with high grades, that the military was their best option.

F.R. attended school in Oakland from 1953 to 1969. "There were only two African Americans in the high tracks at Oakland Tech, (later mayor) Lionel Wilson and his brother. Otherwise we were all together at the bottom."

S.M. attended Oakland Tech. during the same time period and was tracked out of college-prep math. Although she has earned a master's degree in English and is remarkably effective with students of all ethnicities, she cannot become a permanent teacher because she has not passed the math portion of the teacher tests.

UNDEMOCRATIC REPRESENTATION: School boards and superintendents continued to be entirely white, whereas the school population was nearly 50 percent African American.

FACILITIES: Students of color were more frequently housed in portables. In schools with a majority of white students, the average number of portables was two. In schools with a majority of black students, the average number of portables was eleven (Edwards, 1968).

SEGREGATION: By 1964, 95 percent of the students attending school in West Oakland were African American, whereas less than 25 percent of the students in the hills and midland schools were children of color.

EMPLOYMENT: Although 50 percent of the children were African American, only about 15 percent of the teachers were African American. I have found no statistics on the percentage of Latino teachers employed during this period, but I do know from interviews with Latino adults that there were no Latino teachers at Jefferson, Hamilton (now Calvin Simmons), and Fremont, the three schools with the largest Latino student bodies.

TEST SCORES: Scores on the STEP (Sequential Test of Education Progress) test at predominantly black schools were less than half the scores in predominantly white schools. Elementary school students, for example, scored 29.9 in predominantly black schools, whereas students in predominantly white schools scored 62.4 on a test of reading (Edwards, p. 25).

LIVING THE BAD OLD DAYS

The story of Norma M. provides an excellent example of segregation and integration as they played out in the lives of twentieth- century children in Northern cities like Oakland.

Norma M's story is similar to those of other West Oakland residents. Her grandmother had worked as a domestic in Texas and moved to Oakland with her husband during the 1940s. He became a longshoreman; she got a job at the Naval Air Station. They bought a house in West Oakland, where Norma and her young family now reside.

Norma started school in West Oakland in the early 1960s at all-black Wilma Manor Elementary. "Our teachers were mostly black. They were friendly and kind, but they were also stern when they needed to be. I felt that I was getting a good education. But my mother saw that the test scores were not as high as the hill schools. So, when my brother got into Monterra through some special program, my mother insisted that I go to nearby Joaquin Miller." (Norma's mother is now deceased, but Norma imagines that this was probably the open enrollment program referred to in Chapter 3.)

"I was the only black student in my third grade class at Joaquin Miller, and my teacher was the only black teacher in the school. She totally favored the white students. She called on them and ignored me. We had high-level and low-level reading groups. I was the ONLY student in the low-level group. So when it was 2:00 and time for the advanced reading group, all the white kids would say 'It's time for you to go home now, Norma.' I was completely alone and isolated. As a black adult I now understand that the teacher must have had struggles of her own, but she did nothing at all to help me make friends. I was called Aunt Jemimah and sometimes 'nigger.'

"My fourth grade teacher was a white lady who cried on the day that George Wallace was shot. I was a child; I figured that George Wallace must have been a wonderful man, since my teacher was crying.

"I had a very good white teacher in sixth grade. She suggested some special tutoring for me. So I left elementary school reading at grade level. But I am a middle-aged woman now and I still struggle with self-esteem issues, because of my experience at Joaquin Miller."

3

"Mississippi West"

Oakland's Civil Rights Movement

FOR MOST NORTHERNERS THE TERM "SCHOOL segregation" creates images of lynch mobs in some distant Southern city. But there are quite a few people who remember when Oakland, California, was called Mississippi West.

This chapter tells the story of school segregation Oakland-style, its impact on the lives of 55,000 children, and the struggle for racial representation.

In 1954 the national NAACP took a shot at the foundations of U.S. segregation by taking its *Brown v. Board of Education* lawsuit all the way to the U.S. Supreme Court. California was presumed to be more liberal than the Southern states, in which the civil rights movement became most intense, but in Oakland black residents were mostly confined to the western section of the city by housing covenants and intimidation; black children were sometimes warned by their parents not to "go past the Lake" into East Oakland for fear of reprisals; and Oakland had never had a single African American school board member or high-level administrator.

Two years after the victorious Supreme Court decision against segregation, Oakland's all-white school board increased Oakland's segregation by spending $40 million from a bond election to build Skyline High School, and then establishing a ten-mile long, two-mile wide attendance boundary which effectively excluded almost every black and Latino student in the city.

In 1959 protests broke out when two black teachers were discharged from McClymonds High School. Four hundred students, the Alameda Central Labor Council, the NAACP, the ACLU, and the teachers union charged racial discrimination because these teachers were protesting educational inequality.

By 1962 two new school board members declared their opposition to Oakland's eighty year history of de facto segregation. Barney Hilburn, the board's first African American member, and Dr. Robert Nolan attacked the board's selection of long-time Oakland administrator Stuart S. Phillips as the new superintendent. Said Nolan, "The majority has elected to reject a number of outstanding possible selections in favor of one that offers expression for their own provincialism and conservatism, and is understandably most like themselves." (*Oakland Tribune*, 1962, April 27, p.1.) Oakland's black community considered Phillips unsympathetic to black issues, and the controversy over his selection began an eight-year struggle over community participation in superintendent selection.

Both Superintendent Stewart Phillips and school board member Lorenzo Hoopes were indignant at assertions made during the early 1960s that the Oakland school system was guilty of segregation and bigotry. Hoopes, responding to a proposal for school boundary changes, said, "I take it as a personal (as well as a collective) affront to be accused of sharing in bigotry." (*Oakland Tribune*, 1963, April 8, p. 1)

In 1964 several dozen community organizations formed the Ad Hoc Committee for Quality Education in Oakland. The NAACP, the Congress of Racial Equality, the Oakland Federation of Teachers, the 7th and 16th Congressional Democratic Clubs, the Mexican American Unity Council, the Ministerial Alliance, the Urban League, the Welfare Rights Organization, the Catholic Interracial Council, and SEDGE (the Sunday Evening Discussion Group on Education) all participated under the leadership of attorney and later board of supervisors member John George. Oakland's civil rights movement was developing so rapidly that the school board felt obliged to negotiate. Members of the board met with eighteen representatives and heard twenty recommendations, including recognition of the Ad Hoc Committee as a bargaining unit; employment of "Spanish-speaking" and "Negro" counselors; free hot lunch programs for all students; due process in the handling of student confidential files and disciplinary actions; equalization of equipment available at various schools; and training of school personnel in intergroup human relations (Superintendent's Bulletin, May 27, 1966, p. 1).

In 1964 the district had 417 "minority teaching positions." In 1968 it had 817 "minority teaching positions" out of approximately 4,000 teaching positions. This meant that the "improved" proportion of minority teachers was less than 20 percent black in a district where the students were 60 percent black (Phillips, 1968).

And by 1968, the segregation of schools remained. Skyline was 83.8 percent white and Castlemont, less than five miles away, was 81 percent black. The school board adamantly refused to change the school boundaries. Their only concession was to institute an "open enrollment" policy which allowed less than 1 percent of the students to attend schools outside their district.

OAKLAND'S CIVIL RIGHTS MOVEMENT, PART II

These conditions produced an Oakland Civil Rights movement which was extraordinarily broad. The Community Coordinating Committee, for example, which was initiated by the Black Caucus in November of 1969, included thirty-three different organizations: the NAACP, the League of Women Voters, the Baptist Ministers Union, the Black Panthers, the Filipino Coalition, both teachers unions, the Jewish Community Relations Council, and a host of other groups.

In addition to its breadth, this movement exhibited enormous flexibility, using tactics which ranged from elections and community meetings to picketing, sit-ins, and arrests. When the board rebuffed community participation in school district affairs, the Black Caucus established a system of committees paralleling the school board committees and chaired by such dignitaries as U.C. professor Andrew Billingsley. When the school board failed to involve them in superintendent selection, they sent their own representatives to Trenton, New Jersey, to interview one of the candidates.

These protests caused the school district to address some racial issues more seriously. In 1969 the board unanimously adopted a policy requiring that the work force hired to construct Martin Luther King School should reflect, as closely as possible, the racial makeup of the city's population (*Oakland Tribune*, 1969, Oct. 8, p. 1). At the same meeting they approved the hiring of a "school-community human relations assistant" to work with the principals at each high school. The process for hiring was as significant as the position itself. The board agreed to community participation. Each position would be filled by a committee consisting of three school administrators and three neighborhood representatives in each of the six high school attendance zones.

The black community had had no voice in choosing the superintendent for one hundred years. When Stuart Phillips resigned as Oakland superintendent, the Black Caucus, with its thirty-eight member organizations, was determined to change this. A school board meeting in early 1969 was attended by three hundred citizens. Black Caucus chair Paul Cobb presented demands for a citizens' selection committee representing the racial composition of the district's students, which was about 56 percent black (Mitchell, 1969). Cobb declared to the school board and the assembled demonstrators that the board would not be allowed to adjourn until it fulfilled its agreement to involve the community in the selection of the new superintendent. Within eight minutes the Oakland police appeared. They beat and maced a dozen demonstrators and arrested five leaders, including the president of the Teacher's Union, the chair of the local NAACP, and the chair of the CORE (the Congress of Racial Equality).

Two days before the historic school board meeting the Black Caucus had picketed the Oakland Safeway headquarters, where school board president Lorenzo Hoopes was employed as vice-president (*Oakland Tribune*, 1960, June 6, p. 1). The board appointed two black representatives to the selection committee but rejected fuller community participation. Then the board ignored its own selection committee and offered the superintendency to Las Vegas school administrator James Mason. But community protests forced Mason to resign before he had even started work (Classroom Teacher, Oct. 3, 1969).

The school board tried again. In October they selected Dr. Ercell Watson of Trenton, New Jersey. This time they selected an African American but once again they had ignored community involvement. Community organizer and Black Caucus chair Paul Cobb argued that the board was attempting to pit Watson against the black community. "You offered him a big salary but you didn't tell him that you wanted a quiet operator to handle problems behind the scenes."

The trial of the Oakland Five, those arrested at the June school board meeting, began. But many Oaklanders believed that the school board, not the Oakland Five, had acted illegally. A remarkable collection of elected officials and labor and community organizations joined the Oakland Five Defense Committee. State senator Nick Petris, assemblyman Willie Brown, the Northern District Council of the International Longshore Workers Union (ILWU), and Richard Hongisto, the president of the San Francisco Law Enforcement Group, were only a few of the dozens of names which joined the original Black Caucus membership in forming the Oakland Five Defense Committee. An article in the *Catholic Voice* explained the political context of their defense:

> These events concern what the defendants—and many other Oakland citizens—view as a deliberate violation of the law by the Oakland School Board in its admitted failure to follow its own declared procedure for selecting a superintendent of Schools. It was a violation for which they held little hope of being rectified either by the School Board or in the courts. (Close, 1970, p. 1)

The board also lost money because of the arrests. The Central Labor Council decided to withdraw labor support from the school board's June 3 school tax ballot measure, after the arrest of Teachers Union president David Creque, who was one of the Oakland Five. The ballot measure was defeated by a two-to-one margin, "a tangible indication of a loss of community confidence in the Board" (Oakland Federation of Teachers, July 28, 1969 flier).

Oakland Tech. student body president Bernard Nunley had been beaten by police at a May 20 school board meeting, and the Oakland Student Alliance called for high school students to attend the trial each day at 600 Washington Street. "These men are the leaders in the fight for better education in Oakland" (Oakland Student Alliance flier, February 1970).

Community supporter and parent Lorna Jones spent every day of the eleven-week trial in court supporting the defendants. Asked why whites such as herself would put so much energy into defending five men who had been arrested for civil rights issues, she responds, "Many of us thought it was a put up job. Many people thought it was not justifiable for them to be arrested. The School Board wanted them arrested, and we thought they should have dropped the charges, but they refused. The trial was also a terrible waste of money."

Lorna grew up in Ontario, Canada, and moved to Oakland in 1956. She knew no people of color as a child. She married in 1958, and when her daughter was born, she was determined to provide her with multiracial experiences. She joined New Year Callers, a group which visited the homes of people from different ethnicities on the Sunday after New Year's.

Lorna's personal history tells much about the political evolution of whites who joined Oakland's civil rights movement: "I became involved in the League of Women Voters, because I asked my neighbor where all our tax money was going. She couldn't answer, but she told me to look up the League, an organization I had never heard of. We did not focus on Civil Rights at that time, but other issues often led us to the Civil Rights issues. My husband was also an Oakland teacher. Both of those things got me involved in the Oakland Five case."

Public opposition was so massive that the school board began an earnest search for a superintendent who would be accepted by the black community and eventually employed Dr. Marcus Foster, the first African American ever to lead a major urban school district.

Foster had served as associate superintendent of the Philadelphia schools and as principal of both the Catto and the Gratz schools in Philadelphia. At Gratz he organized what was then an unorthodox but successful approach to lowering the dropout rate. Foster organized a campaign in which he went with teachers, parents, and other students to knock on the doors of dropouts and persuade them to come back. In an interesting precursor to Oakland's later ebonics issue, Foster expressed the following view on language development for black children: "When you say, 'I don't like your language' to a child, what he hears, since language is an extension of his personality is 'I don't like you.' What I'm talking about here is not crushing the child but leading him through a succession of experiences..." (Rafsky, 1970)

Immediately upon his appointment, Foster met with members of the Black Caucus, who warned him that he was venturing into a "political jungle." He asserted that he would have preferred community groups having a direct say in his hiring, but looking to the future said, "If activism resulted in my presence here, that's a positive thing." On the trial of the Oakland Five, which was still occurring, he said, "I don't think people should be punished for bringing about positive ends....Abject apathy is harder to deal with." (Zane, 1970, p. 1)

Beginning with their victory over the superintendency, school activists and community leaders began trying to change the entrenched discriminatory practices described in the preceding section. Foster was killed by the Symbionese Liberation Army only a year after his appointment, and was replaced by Ruth Love, another respected African American educator. Bureaucratic regulation ensured that the effort to dismantle discrimination would be a long process, and within twenty years a new challenge arose for the African American elected officials whose children made up a majority of the school district population. The successful opposition to this challenge is reported in the next chapter.

4

Civil Rights and State Takeovers

A Diverse Oakland School Board Defeats an Attempted State Takeover in 1988

THE TASKS OF THE NEWLY INTEGRATED SCHOOL BOARDS

As African Americans were elected to the Oakland school board they faced civil rights tasks in the following seven areas: 1) the use of money. In the pre-1960s era almost all contracts went to white-owned companies for everything from construction to accounting, legal services, and food service. Although the city might have supported civil rights in the abstract, any particular contractor felt that he had a right to continued access to the school district's multimillion dollar budget. 2) hiring. As already described, the vast majority of Oakland teachers were white and monolingual. This was both a job issue and an education issue. Yet it was not easily remedied.

Credential laws, personnel office procedures, and individual schools had processes in place which maintained this situation. 3) curriculum. The curriculum came from textbook publishers, state guidelines, and teacher inclination. All of these were dominated by whites. 4) age-old practices and structures such as tracking, ability grouping, testing, and large factory-model high schools. 5) nearly universal U.S. assumptions about learners, including the idea that many black children used "bad" grammar and came from dysfunctional homes. These assumptions led to a variety of classroom practices and community relationships which alienated the schools from the children who attended them. 6) school facilities and atmosphere. 7) financial stability of the school district. If the new school boards could not balance their budgets, their control of the school district would be lost no matter how important their educational and civil rights initiatives might be.

All of these were addressed to some extent by the integrated school boards which were created as a result of the civil rights struggles described in earlier chapters. In the midst of working on these issues, the Oakland district faced three major new hurdles: whites and more middle-class families were leaving the city, which meant that the average Oakland student had fewer family resources and far more educational needs. "Proposition 13" drastically cut the funding available to California schools. And the State of California began far more regulation and intervention, including an attempt to forcibly take over the district in 1988.

The school board's efforts to deal with the seven areas elaborated above will be discussed in detail in later chapters, but it is important first to understand state takeovers as a national issue and the first attempted takeover in Oakland provides a provocative and interesting example.

TAKING OVER URBAN SCHOOL DISTRICTS: A NATIONAL PHENOMENON

Schools in the U.S. have traditionally been governed by locally elected school boards. Membership on these boards was mostly white and business oriented from the early 1920s through the early 1970s (Tyack, 1974). As described earlier, the Civil Rights movement changed this. In some cities, like Oakland, school board membership began to reflect the composition of the student population, which was approximately 60 percent African American, 25 percent Asian and Latino, and 15 percent white by the late 1980s.

However, during the same late 1980s period, state governments, which were still dominated by white elites, began taking over or disbanding the newly integrated school boards. Between 1988 and 2004, state governments have dismissed the elected school board or taken over its role, either temporarily or permanently, in Baltimore, Chicago, Compton, Detroit, Jersey City, Newark, Philadelphia, and other cities. The districts generally enroll mostly black and Latino students; many of the school district officials are African American.

In most cases the population of the city did not vote to give up its local board, and in some cases, public opposition to the takeover has been intense. For example, Whyatt Mondesire, president of the local NAACP, led a coalition which attacked the Philadelphia takeover by arguing that its ultimate goal was privatization. "The people behind this are more interested in making sure their company stays profitable on Wall Street than in the education of black, Latino and white school children. It would lead to profit-making on the backs of our 210,000, mostly black, students." (American Teacher, 2002)

The teachers union president in Compton, E. Marie Truby, said their takeover was "sort of like a dictatorship" and West Contra Costa school board member Patricia Player complained about the fact that her district will be paying for a loan plus interest to the state until 2017. Why should the district be paying interest to another public entity? "It's very vindictive from a taxpayer's point of view," said Player (Katz, 2003, p. 1).

Initiators of the various takeovers have generally cited test scores and financial crisis as the reasons. But it is reasonable to ask, "Why is the urban school board the only elected entity which loses all its policy making and programmatic functions because of budget deficits?" Every level of state and federal government was in deficit in 2003. Why did no one propose turning the White House over to the United Nations?

Furthermore, 12 percent of the U.S. population is African American but only 2 percent of its elected officials are African American, and a large portion of the 2 percent are school board members. Thus, to remove the power of school boards is to further disenfranchise African Americans as a group.

THE FIRST ATTEMPTED TAKEOVER OF OAKLAND SCHOOLS

One of the early cases of attempted takeover occurred in 1988 in Oakland. This case is important for the following reasons: 1) it was defeated by organized opposition in the city; 2) it played out as an interesting example of the principles elaborated by critical race theory; 3) the local school board took important civil rights actions in the fifteen years following its defeat of the state takeover.

This section will analyze this first attempted takeover, looking at the resistance and its results, and the interplay of institutional and personal racism which shaped both the attempted takeover and the resistance to it.

In 1988, my son was a student in the Oakland schools and I was teaching English. At the time, even though the State of California had a huge budget surplus, its school funding was among the lowest in the nation. Oakland's funding was especially low, even by paltry California standards. During the 1988–89 school year, for example, Oakland received only $2,907 per student as compared to the county average of $3,259 per student (City schools fall short, 1989). We were angry. Many of our school buildings were portables left over from World War II; the state had failed to credential enough teachers, which meant that many of our classrooms were staffed by substitutes; little six-year-olds were trying to learn reading in classrooms of thirty-two children; and we were told to prepare for state intervention and more cuts.

I joined with other parents and community members in a coalition to fight looming budget cuts and the takeover of the school district by the State of California. Our first action was to organize a Speak Out, which was attended by 150 parents and several politicians. We focused on the state government, demanding that they use the state budget surplus for schools. At the end of the Speak Out, a man began circulating a petition against the local school board, a petition which he ultimately used to organize a confrontation against the board. I was disturbed, because I felt he was hijacking a meeting organized about state funding and turning it against the local board.

"They don't have any money," I argued.

"Oh, yes, they do. They should cut from the top," he replied.

"They could cut out the whole top, and there still would not be enough money," I said. "And if they did what you suggest, they would go bankrupt, and we would end up with a state trustee, which would completely disenfranchise Oakland." Despite my arguments, he began to mobilize parents for a confrontation at the next school board meeting.

No one on the school board would have argued that they had created wonderful schools by 1988. Despite their supposed legal authority, and although they could point to progress on equity issues, they continued to be "outsiders" confronting a vast local and state bureaucracy. The state bureaucracies insisted that their regulations were "color-blind," even though they produced color-coded results.

When I arrived at the school board meeting at which the budget cuts were being discussed, I found several hundred parents, many of them shouting at the school board. My stomach churned as I watched one speaker after another belittle and degrade school board members whose own children attended schools far more deprived than those attended by the speakers' children. I sat in the audience among white liberals whose children constituted only 7 percent of the district's population. They berated the African American school board majority, using the slogans of the civil rights movement. "We are the people," they said.

Something was wrong here. I had always identified protests with progress, but it seemed to me that these protesters were on the wrong side.

THE STATE PUSHES FOR A TRUSTEE

Under California law the only basis for state intervention was fiscal insolvency. The Oakland school board was not seeking a state loan, but some public officials began talking about state intervention anyway. State schools superintendent Bill Honig had already interfered extensively in the Oakland schools and had expressed the desire to "get Oakland under a trustee." Elihu Harris was running for mayor and his campaign manager, Larry Tramatola (a former employee of Honig), had conducted a poll indicating that Harris had little name recognition and suggested that moving for state intervention would get his name in the papers. The one remaining white member of the school board agreed to push for a state loan without consulting the other board members.

Those who favored state takeover—State Superintendent Honig, mayoral candidate Harris, and school board member Jordan—made the following arguments:

First, they argued that accepting a loan and a trustee would be preferable to making budget cuts.

Second, Honig argued that the African American school board members did not care about African American children. They cared only about black jobs. "I wish somebody would care about black children as much as they do about black administrators," he fumed. "They just care about jobs." (Put the heat on school leaders, 1989)

Third, they said that the school district was filled with corruption and nepotism, and presented the following evidence: 1) school board member Darlene Lawson had a daughter who was employed as a custodian; and 2) a school district employee, Raymond Crump, was accused of stealing school district property including power tools, toilet seats, and typewriters.

Finally, County Superintendent William Berck also supported a state trustee, but his reasoning was more straightforward. He considered the school board too responsive to the community. He said that there was only one way to balance the budget, which was to cut programs and lay off staff. A state trustee would, he said, help the board to "make the hard decisions."

Those who opposed trusteeship (a majority of the school board; the Ad Hoc Committee of Parents and Teachers, which was organized to oppose trusteeship; and other community organizations) responded in three ways. To begin, they felt the trustee would actually create a need for greater cuts, because the district would be responsible for paying the trustee's salary plus interest on the state loan. In addition, the district would lose all control over *which* cuts to make, because the trustee would have absolute power. Although Oakland had many people of color in elective and administrative positions, the state government had almost none. So Oakland's progress in black representation would be removed by the absolute power of a Sacramento-appointed trustee.

In addition, half the students in Oakland schools were African American, the school district was the second largest employer, and many working-class black people worked for the school district, because it was the only available job. To contrast the educational interests of black children with their parents' need for employment seemed ludicrous to many. Finally, many believed that the corruption investigations and trusteeship move reflected the racial bias of those business interests who disliked the post–civil rights influence of African Americans in the city of Oakland. School board member Darlene Lawson said, "It seems to me it's a power trip for the downtown business interests, who are mostly white." (Battle lines drawn, 1989) Oakland's most prominent African American minister, J. Alfred Smith, also referred to an "invisible power structure: which includes some corporate leaders that want to make sure parents—especially black parents—are not involved in deciding the future of the Oakland schools." (Pastor J. Alfred Smith, 1989, p. 2)

Fourth, the Oakland school board considered community responsiveness to be part of its mandate. They maintained such relatively expensive programs as small elementary schools and district-funded child care centers because they believed these programs to be in the best interest of children. They opposed a trustee precisely because they did not want the "hard decisions" made by the state. The public battle was intense. Bill Honig and his allies pushed ahead with a two-pronged strategy: demanding that Oakland make no budget cuts (thus ensuring bankruptcy and the need for a trustee) and charging corruption, often with thinly veiled racial references. At one point Honig attacked Pastor J. Alfred Smith with the charge that he too "only cared about black jobs."

I was personally disturbed because many of the white folks battling the African American school board members identified with the same "progressives" with whom I identified. These were the people who listened to Pacifica Radio and read Noam Chomsky. I recognized that I needed to rethink the entire relationship of Bay Area white progressives to the black and Latino communities. I could not assume that the most acceptable position among white progressives would necessarily be the antiracist position.

Parent Lou Ann Aaberg, attorney Walter Riley, and I organized the Ad Hoc Committee of Teachers and Parents and soon allied with longtime activists Kay Tillman, Gracie Johnson, and many others. Parents and students rallied in front of the state building and in Sacramento to demand "No trustee" and "Use the state's $2.5 billion budget surplus to finance schools." We spoke at meetings and gave interviews to the press. We proposed in June that a combination of $3.5 million in administrative cuts plus a $9 million Oakland share of the state's $2.5 billion surplus would go far toward balancing the budget. Mayor Lionel Wilson and the black ministerial alliance opposed the trusteeship proposal. Even the relatively affluent Montclair Greater Oakland Democratic Club would not vote for a trustee. Said club president Bill Rowen, "It's one of the situations where the cure is worse than the illness." (MGO tables Harris bill, 1989, p. 5)

When the school board voted in mid-August to rehire seventy-seven teachers at a cost of $3.9 million, all the experts predicted loudly that a trustee was inevitable. Said U.C. education policy professor James Guthrie, "By taking this step they knew they were inviting state intervention. It was an organizational death wish." (Oakland school board's face-saving decision, 1989) Honig, who had promised in March to get Oakland under a trustee, was declaring on August 17 that a trustee was now "inevitable." Guthrie elaborated further, "They (the school board) may have governmentally emasculated themselves, but some of them are still politically wise. They know how the world works and are mindful of the consequences."

MAKING THE WORLD WORK DIFFERENTLY

But Guthrie underestimated the determination of two board members to make the world work differently. Sylvester Hodges and Darlene Lawson shocked the city at a late August board meeting by announcing that they had arranged to issue $10 million worth of "Certificates of Participation," thus making a state loan unnecessary and saving $450,000 in interest which would have been required for a state loan.

State Superintendent Honig declared that he would block the sale of certificates (Battle lines drawn, 1989), but Hodges and Lawson had done their homework carefully. Other districts had already used this method of financing, and the board members had carefully worked through the necessary procedures before announcing the plan. Said district business manager John Hills, "The people who say we are in a grave situation are just misreading things, wittingly or unwittingly. This is trashing time for Oakland." (Battle lines drawn, 1989) Harris proceeded with his trusteeship AB2525 bill, but since the strategizing of Hodges and Lawson had made a loan unnecessary, the bill seemed even more transparently political. In the end Harris's bill imposed only an "advisory trustee."

One year later, the neighboring Richmond school district, a district with similar economic and ethnic demographics, went broke and was forced to accept the $10 million loan originally slated for Oakland. They were also forced to lay off hundreds of teachers and cut the salaries of those teachers who remained. Today, more than a decade later, that district, now called West Contra Costa County, has not yet recovered financially. Interest and fees on the loan were so high that the loan will not be repaid and local control restored until 2018.

In contrast, Oakland did not lay off teachers or cut salaries. And by the time Sylvester Hodges ended his tenure as chair of the district's Budget and Finance Committee, the school district had achieved Standard & Poor's highest bond rating and had accumulated a substantial cushion of reserves (Kelling, Northcross, & Nobriga Financial Services Memorandum, 1999). In addition, the board took a number of nationally noteworthy policy steps in the period following the 1988 victory against takeover.

IS IT ABOUT RACE?

As I participated in these events, I began to see a web of race-related institutional and personal actions that affected Oakland's leaders and students profoundly. Racism was not a simple set of racial stereotypes; it was deeply imbedded in every aspect of the school system and its actors. And its antidote was not an old-fashioned list of civil rights demands.

In *Education and Inequality*, Caroline Hodges Persell analyzes educational inequality by dissecting its operation at four levels: societal, institutional, interpersonal, and intrapsychic (Persell, 1979). Her framework provides a useful breakdown for examining the multiple ways that race in America impacted the school district during its 1988–89 school year.

SOCIETAL AND INSTITUTIONAL INEQUALITY: THE SCHOOL DISTRICT AND ITS MULTIMILLION-DOLLAR BUDGET

Former board member Sylvester Hodges echoes the critical race theorists in arguing that school district decisions are often rooted in property relations. He laughs at the idea that the decisions politicians and bureaucrats make are primarily motivated by "the children." This "follow the money" analysis is probably true of most American institutions; but for a school district that is 60 percent African American (1989 figure), in a country where most black people have little wealth, the right to make decisions about the expenditure of a $220 million budget takes on added significance. The condition and representation of black people in America has always been shaped by white capital, from slavery through sharecropping and Northern industrialization, and fair political representation has long been denied.

In fact, there have been only two times in U.S. history when African Americans have had anything close to fair political representation. After the Civil War victory against slavery, African Americans won political representation in the Reconstruction South. Sixteen were elected to Congress, and six hundred served in state legislatures in the South. In total, there were about two thousand black elected officials in the post–Civil War South. "This was the most visible and revolutionary gain of Radical Reconstruction." (Jackson, 1996, p. 179)

But no group of public officials in American history experienced as many violent attacks as these black elected officials. Fifty-six were killed. Others were shot at and forced from their homes. The power of black elected officials posed an economic threat to wealthy whites.

The second expansion of black representation followed the civil rights movement of the 1960s and 1970s. In 1970, there were 362 black elected officials on school boards and other education bodies across the country. By 1990, there were 1,645 black officials in these positions (Statistical Abstract of the U.S., No. 452).

Despite Oakland's large black population, the first African American school board member was not seated in Oakland until 1958. By 1988, a majority of the school board's seven members were black, a number which accurately represented the city's majority black population.

Sylvester Hodges, elected in 1984, believed that the district's budget held the key to both better education and better black representation. He began asking for detailed reports on hiring and contracting procedures. He asked for a report on the percentages of minority and white businesses with which the district contracted as compared to the percentages offering services in a particular area. He asked the personnel office for regular reports on the numbers and percentages of non-white teachers and administrators being employed. Hodges believed that the district was wasting money on legal and accounting services, and that a greater portion of these services could be handled in-house. This change upset the corporate legal and accounting giants whose services and contract were replaced through these actions of the school board. So state takeover of the district by a trustee was seen by some businesses as a way back to "normalcy," where white business, sometimes with a few token black employees, automatically had the upper hand in contracting.

INTERPERSONAL DYNAMICS OF RACE: WHO IS THE VICTIM?

White progressives tend to talk about the "wealthy" as those with millions of dollars, and then to treat everyone else as part of the "middle class" or some other undifferentiated set of regular folks. This approach obscures the dramatic differences in wealth that occur even among "regular folks" because of the history of American racism. In fact, the *median* white family holds *five times* the accumulated assets of the median black family (Oliver & Shapiro, 1995). As Dalton Conley points out, black families actually graduate their children from high school at a slightly higher rate than white families at comparable wealth levels. But slavery, sharecropping, Jim Crow laws, and discriminatory housing and lending laws have prevented black people from accumulating assets (Conley, 1999).

This does not put all black people in a separate social class from all white people, but it does mean that many African Americans have substantially greater need for accessible jobs and education than do many whites. The white parent activists ignored how their racial position was reflected in their actions. In general, they congratulated each other for the fact that they "kept their children in public school" and considered this a mark of their egalitarian outlook. As a reward they believed that their children were entitled to "quality" education and believed themselves to be the injured parties when the school board attempted to make cuts to avoid the imposition of a trustee.

Some of these activists mentally pasted their experiences as student activists onto an urban school district. They made the following analogy: We were activists fighting the Vietnam War and the "system." Now we are injured parents fighting for our children and the "system" is the school board. The analogy seemed sensible but it was not (Grillo & Wildman, 1991). In fact, many of the former student activists had become upper-middle-class lawyers, doctors, and business executives, and the school board consisted of less affluent black parents. The African American board members, in attempting to represent their communities, were obliged to recognize the likely loss of both representation and employment that the imposition of a state trustee would bring about.

INTERPERSONAL DYNAMICS OF RACE: SAVING BLACK CHILDREN FROM THEIR ELDERS

Some of white America maintains a myth about the condition of black people. Ignoring the fact that unequal wealth, created by a history of slavery and Jim Crow, creates different social conditions for many African Americans, some whites act as though black people need to be saved from themselves.

This aspect of racism caused some white observers, including reporters and academics, to see the increasing number of black administrators and policy makers in Oakland not as a civil rights victory, but instead as "corruption" and "nepotism." Since black adults could not possibly be the competent organizers of instruction for black children, they must, by this logic, have been hired because of cronyism. In fact, there is evidence that the best instruction for black youngsters has been organized by black adults (Delpit, 1996). The historically black colleges, for example, graduate black students at a considerably higher rate than comparable white institutions.

THE INTRAPSYCHIC DYNAMICS OF RACE: THE IMPORTANCE OF LEADERSHIP AND THE POSSIBILITY OF RESISTANCE

The noteworthy part of this story is not the economic and interpersonal racism, because these are universal in America. The remarkable fact is that the move toward state control was defeated.

Persell describes the "intrapsychic" aspect of structural inequality as one in which the victim—a black student, a working-class white parent, an Asian school board member—internalizes the analysis of the broader social system and sees himself or herself as deficient in some respect. This battering of the internal psyche occurs among the elected representatives of marginalized groups as surely as it does among parents and students. Under the bombardment of press reports, investigations, and organized protests, it is difficult for anyone to maintain balance and direction (Persell, 1979).

Sylvester Hodges was the critical figure in overcoming this intrapsychic barrage. His strategies were simple but effective. He ran around Oakland's three-mile lake several times a week. He used his knowledge of wrestling and history to develop strategies. And he ignored the negative hype. "When acquaintances began to believe the press reports, I stayed away from them. I went over to my mother's house instead. She would say, 'I know Sylvester. He's a financial conservative, and he's doing the right thing. You'll see.'" (Hodges, 2001)

In addition, he avoided the political pitfall that has seized many politicians in Oakland: favors owed to more powerful politicians and business leaders. Since service on the city council or the school board is considered a part-time job, some grassroots council and school board members have taken jobs for city government or for more powerful politicians, and this has made them highly subject to pressure. Hodges maintained his employment outside of Oakland, and cultivated his base primarily in his own district, whose voters were mostly working class African Americans. This made him somewhat less vulnerable to the demand that he abandon his principles to support someone else's agenda.

AFTERMATH

Oakland maintained its autonomy for fifteen years following the 1988 attempted takeover. This meant that: 1) the school district saved thousands of dollars in looming trustee fees and interest; 2) the school district ended up in better financial health than the city itself or the surrounding school districts; and 3) the district maintained the leadership of the African American majority, which produced a number of historic innovations.

Although the newspapers projected that the "corruption" in the district would result in fifty arrests, including top administrators and board members, none of these arrests ever occurred. The only conviction to result from the entire series of events described above was a plea bargain by the person who "stole" the abandoned school lockers to use in his gym. Ironically, one of the leaders of the takeover attempt, State Superintendent Bill Honig, was himself arrested and convicted a few years later for using public funds to finance his wife's parent organizing campaign.

WHAT DIFFERENCE DID IT MAKE TO MAINTAIN LOCAL CONTROL: EQUITY INITIATIVES

In the fifteen years which followed the 1988 defeat of state takeover the Oakland school board was a leader among Northern cities in asserting new policies in civil rights. In the ten years between the 1989 defeat of state takeover and the next attempted takeover in 1999, the school board accomplished the following:

1. A partial end to tracking: In the 1980s the Oakland school board passed a resolution abolishing tracking. It abolished Terman's third track, the "remedial track," which had previously condemned students to a permanent label as substandard learner. The post-1980 school boards insisted that the new career academies would prepare all students to meet college requirements if they chose to attend.

2. Furthermore, many school board members supported the initiative by an independent black organization to seek relief from the courts for the de facto tracking which continued to exist. The district, under the leadership of its first Asian superintendent, entered into a voluntary resolution plan for undoing the effects of tracking on the achievement of African American students.

3. The possibility of moving toward equity required an independent school district which, in turn, required financial stability. By 1998 the more representative school boards, with leadership from board president Sylvester Hodges, had achieved the following:

   a) In short-term debt, the district achieved the highest possible rating from Standard & Poor's, SP1+.

   b) For bonds, the district purchased insurance which raised the rating on the bonds to the highest ratings available: Standard & Poor's AAA and Moody's AAA (Kelling, Northcross, & Nobriga, 1999).

4. Oakland became the district with the most ethnically representative teaching force in California (Keleher & Libero, 1999).

5. Employment in general: throughout the U.S., student academic achievement is tied to the employment of their parents. It is no small achievement to provide fair employment to the non-white citizens of the city, since they are often the parents of the students.

6. It approved one of the first charter schools to focus on non-affluent youngsters, the Oakland Charter Academy, which enrolls primarily Latinos.

7. It rejected an intense push by for-profit charter schools, including Edison.

8. It employed the first Asian American female as superintendent of any major district in the United States.

9. It was the largest district in California to reject a state-adopted social studies series that had been condemned by every major civil rights and community organization for its racial insensitivity (Martinez, 1995).

10. It undertook measures that are now internationally applauded for supporting the language needs of African American students (Baugh, 2000; Perry & Delpit, 1998).

OTHER TAKEOVERS

The state of Michigan took over the Detroit schools in 1999. The takeover law was written to expire in 2004. Under the takeover the gap between student scores in Detroit and other districts actually widened. Remarkably, those who took over the district began making the same arguments which they had earlier rejected and called "excuses," such as the argument that student poverty led to the lowered test scores.

In 2004, Detroit voters were asked to pass "Measure E," which would have allowed the mayor to appoint the district superintendent. There would be an elected school board, but they would not have the power to make contracts. Detroit voters rejected "Measure E" by 65 percent, which means that the Detroit schools will again have an elected board in 2006.

CONCLUSIONS

In the early part of the 20th century, school reformers made drastic changes in the governance of urban school systems, arguing for factory-model schools appropriately oriented to the abilities of individual students, with those abilities defined by a test maker who had a racially biased view of the world. The resulting school boards were dominated by elites who supported a vast system of testing, tracking, and de facto segregation (Tyack, 1974; Cubberly, 1916). Now the takeover of urban systems is again supported by the argument that the system reorganization will meet student needs. Although there is no evidence for this contention, issues of civil rights are again turned upside down (Chambers, 2002). Take over proponents are arguing that the civil rights issue in this case involves reduction of the "achievement gap" between black and white students, which will be better achieved through state takeover. Progressives have often failed to fight the takeovers, because they have ignored both the multidimensional nature of civil rights in an urban system and the logical trap of calling for equalized test scores. Civil rights are not only about education; they are also about democracy and control over the large public budgets expended in schools. Furthermore, the call for equalized test scores ignores the nature of the tests, which were created with the purpose of showing students of different ethnicities and social classes to have different "abilities."

Critical race scholars in the field of law argue that "the law's much-vaunted neutrality and objectivity are not just unattainable ideals; they are harmful fictions that cloak the role of the law in subverting racial equity and ensuring white privilege." (Hamilton, 2002) Oakland's experience seems to indicate that this generalization is equally applicable to the structures of the U.S. educational system. And in this context, Oakland's history of resistance is especially noteworthy.

Academics and activists seeking educational justice may wish to consider the following:

1. School governance is a messy but critical aspect of civil rights. Rather than treating locally elected school boards as just one more enemy, teachers unions and parent organizations may wish to ally with local school boards to maintain local control, even while continuing to struggle with them over issues of concern to their constituents.

2. Thus far the courts have allowed school district takeovers. However, commonsense reasoning about equal rights leads many to conclude that there is some denial of constitutional protection when the only populations who lose their right to elected school boards are populations which are mostly black, Latino, and Asian.

3. The societal rationale for removing elected representation of school boards is rooted in the idea that there is "colorblind" justice. According to this logic, all schools, all children, all curriculums are the same, and therefore all standards, all tests, all regulations, and all systems should work the same, and school boards should be held to the same "standard." This is questionable on its face, given that most of the wealthiest Americans send their children to a system of elite private schools which face none of the regulations imposed on public schools (Cookson & Persell, 1989). But even if we consider only the public schools, the notion that all public schools are the same and colorblind is a "harmful fiction." The issue of teacher supply is just one example. Teachers, generally middle-class and white, are likely to migrate to more middle-class and white school districts once they are credentialed. Therefore, continuing to credential mostly white and middle-class teachers, under rules which are established by the state with little input from urban districts, ensures that public schools will never have an adequate supply of teachers, and students

will therefore never receive the same instruction. This is only one of a myriad of issues where a critical look at the underlying structures makes clear the "blaming the victim" mentality inherent in school district takeovers and laws such as No Child Left Behind.

4. Improvement in policies on issues of race has occurred during periods of struggle, when the fiction of color-blind justice has been unmasked. Progress on democratic control of urban districts, on credentialing and funding, and on every other education issue seems more likely to occur through renewed social movements than through endless policy debates.

5

Curriculum and Structures

Social Studies Textbooks, Tracking, and Other Issues

IN 1989, THE STATE OF CALIFORNIA ADOPTED a single elementary social studies series published by Houghton-Mifflin. The state adoption meant that each district was expected to use its textbook allocation to purchase the adopted book. The Oakland school board voted 5-2 against purchasing the book, arguing that it presented a racist view of history that implicitly excluded many California students. This battle became the subject of a heated national debate, and I shall return to its content and consequences later in this chapter.

But before the Houghton-Mifflin battle there were dozens of other issues pursued by Oakland's increasingly diverse and equity-minded school boards. As you will recall from the first chapter, Oakland was among the first school districts in the country to be extensively tracked. The school board created a multicultural task force in the late 1980s which proposed a resolution to stop "ability-based" tracking in the district. The resolution was adopted, and the ugliest forms of race- and class-based tracking were ended. But tracking is an excellent example of the implementation difficulties which confront any urban school district. Oakland ended the bottom "remedial" track, but all sorts of extra money and federal funds were attached to the "special ed" and "gifted" categories and special perks for students accompanied such courses as "advanced placement," which continued to be offered.

Nevertheless, Oakland attempted to use the funds in more inclusive ways. They did not generally organize separate "gifted" classes, as some districts have done, and "advanced placement" was generally open to any student who wished to try it.

Among the most difficult of the tracking issues was the question of math placement. For years the unstated assumption was that most Oakland students could not do algebra. Yet, most four-year colleges required algebra for admission. Thus, most Oakland students completed four years of high school without having met the minimum college requirements and often without the information or power to decide otherwise. At one junior high school which I observed closely throughout the early 1980s, the math department scheduled only one section of algebra for a cohort of ninth graders, which was approximately 300 students. Since ninth grade is the year when almost all "college-bound" students take algebra, this meant that 250 ninth graders would automatically be excluded from college by the fact that they were scheduled for general math or pre-algebra, instead of algebra. Challenged by one of the math teachers about this practice, the math chair said the excluded students had not passed the "algebra placement test." This teacher then prepared his eighth graders carefully for the test. A number of them passed but they were then told that their scores were not as high as those of other students and since there was only one section of algebra, they still would not be allowed to take the course. When the eighth-grade teacher angrily challenged the math chairperson, he was told that it was "too late" to change the number of sections and those students would be unlikely to do well in the course anyway. At this point, the teacher urged parents to protest and the math department ultimately added one more section of algebra.

School board members found such practices very difficult to dismantle. Ultimately, one board member, Noel Gallo, himself the father of four Oakland schoolchildren, became so frustrated that he proposed a policy that ALL Oakland ninth graders be immediately enrolled in algebra. The proposal passed the board and the math departments scrambled. There were not enough teachers and the preparation of many students was so poor that they failed the class. It was not, by any means, an optimal arrangement, but it did send a clear signal that the Oakland board expected Oakland students to receive the required preparation for college admission.

One of Oakland's first African American board members, James Norwood, had taken a similar step, when he proposed and passed a resolution that all students were to be taught from textbooks at their own grade level—ninth graders from ninth-grade books, and so on. I remember listening to many conversations at the back of the school board meeting room where teachers whispered about how "ridiculous" and "impossible" such a resolution was, since the students could not read the books anyway. Norwood's response to his critics: "The students may not be able to read the books now, but they'll never be able to read them if they don't even get a chance to see them."

The most clear-cut opportunity to weigh in on national equity issues came with the Oakland school board's 1991

vote on whether to purchase the Houghton-Mifflin social studies series. Proponents of the book argued that the
Houghton-Mifflin series represented a great improvement
in multiculturalism. Whereas the old social studies series
presented Martin Luther King in one paragraph, they said,
the new series expanded his role to three paragraphs.

But opponents were not impressed—they felt that the
book's weaknesses were conceptual and pervasive throughout the series. Native American activists, for example,
questioned the concept of "moving West." This phrasing
presumed the readers of the book to be the descendants
of European immigrants, since the ancestors of Indians,
Mexicans, and Chinese were *not* moving from the East
Coast to the West Coast. Since the descendants of these
groups make up 60 percent of California schoolchildren,
they argued, this European perspective was offensive, inaccurate, and confusing.

The country was so used to reading its history from a
European perspective that many had to think hard even
to understand the criticisms which were being raised. The
Rochester (New York) multicultural project issued a critique of the fifth-grade text. They pointed to the wording
of a section on the cotton gin which said, "Eli Whitney's
time and labor saving invention actually increased the need
for slave labor." Said the critics, "The cotton gin increased
the need for labor, not slave labor. The use of forced labor was a choice which the text presents as essential." In
another spot the fifth-grade text says, "In Daniel Boone's
time, the frontier was the vast unexplored western part of
the country." The critics responded that "This statement
reinforces the Eurocentric stereotype of a barren wilder-
ness waiting to be tamed and settled. Native Americans
had been living and "settled" here for thousands of years
(Waugh, Aug. 10, 1990, p. A1).

The Association of Chinese Teachers (TACT), based in San Francisco, called on the State Board of Education not to adopt Houghton-Mifflin because the books did not meet the state's own requirements in terms of scholarship and accuracy with regard to the Chinese (personal communication from Helen Joe Lew, TACT President, August 23, 1990).

Latina author Elizabeth Martinez noted dozens of objectionable quotations about Latinos. She says that "Resistance to U.S. occupation (of Mexican land) is transformed into sheer criminality." She quotes the Houghton-Mifflin book as follows: "'Joaquin!' they gasped. 'No one felt safe...Who was this Mexican bandit?'"

"Actually," says Martinez, "Anglo miners drove Murietta (like other Latino miners) out of the goldfields after reportedly raping his wife; as a result, he began a guerrilla-like movement that enjoyed widespread support." (Martinez, 1995, p. 108)

African American activist Fred Ellis said textbooks are one of the reasons students drop out of school. "You can't use material that's irrelevant." (Gitlin, 1995, p. 51)

Multiculturalism is sometimes seen as a liberal reform but this multicultural battle was an intense form of social activism (Sleeter, 1996). Scholar Joyce King became a heroine to many when she took the unprecedented step of breaking with the State Curriculum Commission, of which she was a member, to call for rejection of the books. Hundreds rallied at school board meetings; a coalition of nearly a hundred civil rights and education organizations was formed. Liberal author Gary Nash was dispatched to Oakland by the publishers, and then roundly chastised when he addressed the community. The torn loyalties of white "progressives" emerged as white activists attempted to protect author Gary Nash, whom they considered a progressive icon (Nash, 1991).

The book struggle involved money as well as content. California is 11 percent of the U.S. textbook market, and Houghton-Mifflin planned to make over $50 million off the sales.

RACIAL INTERESTS

Oakland activists organized intensively against the books and hundreds appeared at the school board meeting where the final vote was taken. The vote on the board broke down on racial lines. Every black, Asian, or Latino school board member voted against all or part of the books. The one white school board member, who identified herself as a progressive, voted in favor of purchasing all the books.

A white curriculum specialist, who also identified as a progressive, spoke to me after the community confrontation with author Gary Nash. "I felt so bad during that meeting. I felt so bad for Nash," she said. "That could have been any of us ("progressive" whites)."

I was shocked for a moment and then replied, "You must be kidding. He had a choice. He could have acknowledged the faults in the books, instead of defending Houghton-Mifflin. I feel bad for all the kids who have to read these books."

The board member and the curriculum specialist were not the only whites to jump up to Nash's defense. The textbook issue was a dramatic opportunity for those who identified as white progressives to take a stand on issues which had been identified as significant first by a black scholar and then by every major civil rights organization. Former activist and Columbia University professor Todd Gitlin used the Houghton-Mifflin case as the first chapter of his book, *Twilight of Our Common Dreams*, in which he argued individuals like those who campaigned against the social studies series are responsible for the rightward drift of the country because they spend time on something he called "identity politics." He called the books "the most pluralist textbooks ever brought before the state of California," and called the whole struggle against them the "narcissism of small differences." (Bensky, 1995, p. 27) Asked to explain which groups he felt were guilty of bringing division through identity politics he said, "Many of them are so-called racial or ethnic minorities, or groups who are organized around their narrow group interest." (Wattenberg, 1995)

I was involved in the Houghton-Mifflin controversy and saw the events I have described as a disheartening display of the point critical race theorists now make about "interest convergence." Unlike the ebonics issue or even the state takeover, there was no question where non-white organizations and communities stood on Houghton-Mifflin. Yet many of those white leaders who considered themselves "progressive" did not find the insults described by these organizations sufficiently compelling to oppose the books. To endorse the struggle would place them in the uncomfortable position of criticizing someone they considered a fellow white progressive, and they did not consider the book content significant.

In a sympathetic interview conducted by Todd Gitlin, Nash rejected many of the points made by his critics, but some of the points made most forcefully by the coalition of civil rights groups were, in fact, confirmed by Nash himself. The story was told as a European narrative, he agreed. He said he did this because the Europeans had power; he did not address the fact that the book's perspective does not identify European power moving across the country but indicates that this is motion of Americans as a whole. According to Gitlin, Nash was "surprised" when Gitlin told him that the texts included a reference to the "discovery of the New World"; Nash explained that he could not possibly have read all 3,000 pages of the series text when the job was so rushed (Gitlin, 1995). His public defense of a book he had not even read, let alone written, is all the more interesting.

Nash expected support for his position, because he had earlier defended Angela Davis and had written a number of books supporting multicultural history. One wonders why these experiences did not lead him to seek a dialogue with the civil rights advocates criticizing his books. Given only the criticisms with which he agreed, he could have joined the protestors, critiqued the books, and urged Houghton-Mifflin to withdraw them or rewrite them using a multi-racial panel of historians. Nash did none of these things. White racial solidarity won out; Nash and his allies among white progressives spoke in support of Houghton-Mifflin and assisted their free access to the $50 million California market. There were, it is important to note, many whites who did oppose the books, but those identified as "leaders" among white progressives were generally not among them.

THE LONG-TERM IMPACT

The Hayward Unified School district also rejected the Houghton-Mifflin series and developed a different set of curriculum materials. In their request to fund these materials they noted, "By not recommending the adoption of these materials (Houghton-Mifflin), the K–8 committee acknowledged the importance of addressing the underlying ethnic/cultural issues of curriculum perspective and instructional approaches important to the Hayward Education Community." (Hayward Unified School District, 1993) Hayward had already been moving against reliance on textbooks and twenty Hayward teachers had spent several years developing a non-text-based sixth grade social studies curriculum. When the social studies adoption cycle occurred in 1991, Hayward did not even take the Houghton-Mifflin series to its board for a vote (Waugh, May 17, 1992, p. Bl). East Palo Alto and Alum Rock districts rejected the text; Santa Clara bought them but said they would not be used on a daily basis. In Berkeley, like Oakland, the school board vote also broke down along racial lines with both non-Anglos voting against the books. However, in the case of Berkeley the whites outnumbered non-white board members by 3-2.

A group of graduate students surveyed parents at one Oakland elementary school attended by mostly African American students. Of the 110 parents surveyed, 90 percent were aware of the Houghton-Mifflin issue, and 78 percent supported the school board's stance.

Five years after the controversy I approached each of the vendors selling social studies texts at a national education conference. I did not identify myself, except as a conference participant. I asked each vendor whether he or she felt that the Houghton-Mifflin controversy had impacted the way his or her publisher portrayed multicultural issues. Each was aware of the issue and responded vigorously that there had been a major impact. One representative lowered her voice to a confidential tone and shared that "Houghton-Mifflin hasn't changed theirs much at all. Their changes are just cosmetic. But look here at what we have done." She proceeded to show me a dozen sections of their text which used lengthy selections by well-known Latino, Asian, African American, and Native American authors. The fact that the books were written with one voice, that of a European male, was a major complaint against the Houghton-Mifflin series.

6

The "Leave No Teacher" Laws

State and Federal Regulations Mandating a "Highly Qualified" Teaching Force Actually Create Problems for Urban Communities

C URRICULUM MATTERS, BUT NOTHING IN a school district makes as much difference as its teachers. Urban districts have been criticized for years for failing to provide a "qualified" teaching force. The issue is so important and so misunderstood that I will devote the entire chapter to it. What does it mean for a teacher to be qualified? Why do urban districts have a shortage? Whose fault is it? What are the ultimate consequences? And what are the general solutions? The next chapter will be devoted to a particular solution created in Oakland, in spite of the constraints imposed by credentialing laws.

A slightly modified version of this chapter appeared in the journal *Social Justice*, 2005, under the title "The Whitening of the American Teaching Force, a Problem of Racism?"

I begin with a true story, the story of a student without a teacher and, at the same school, a teacher required to leave his students. Then I move on to the state and federal regulations which contribute to this situation.

Nicola attended one of the lowest income high schools in California. She passed algebra and geometry courses required by the state university system she planned to attend. She had five different teachers in each of these courses, because none of the people placed in her classroom met the requirements to be a "highly qualified" teacher, and so each could only be placed as a substitute and then removed after a few weeks. The teachers who assigned grades at the end of the semester rightly concluded that Nicola should not be penalized for having no permanent teacher, and so they gave her a passing grade. However, although she has a good grade point average in her college courses, she will soon be kicked out of college, because she has not been able to pass the required college math exam in the required time.

Does this sound like an argument in support of the "highly qualified" teacher provisions of No Child Left Behind? On the contrary, in this case, NCLB and related state regulations caused the problem; they did not correct it. Requiring schools to have "highly qualified teachers" does not create the teachers, nor does it keep them in place in the schools where they are most needed.

At the same high school attended by Nicola, Mr. Anderson taught algebra for a few weeks and was then removed, because he did not have the equivalent of a college math major. I observed Mr. Anderson in his classroom. Both the students' comments and my observation confirmed that the students were comprehending his algebra instruction. When he was removed from the class after a month, he was replaced by a succession of day-to-day substitutes who had less teaching experience and less math preparation than he had. Of course, it would be desirable for Mr. Anderson to have a math major, but since no teacher with a math major was available, it is irresponsible for state and federal regulation to mandate the removal of a relatively effective teacher. A better and less expensive option would be to leave Mr. Anderson in his classroom and require that he take an advanced math course each semester at a local college.

Although federal and state legislation, including the law called "No Child Left Behind," supposedly aim for "high quality" teachers, they have actually created a situation where there are no teachers at all for many of the lowest income students.

The credentialing situation is perhaps the clearest example of federal and state regulation preventing urban communities, including Oakland, from creating stable and livable schools. In this chapter I will explore a different analysis of the teacher diversity and teacher shortage issue. I will then report on Oakland's response.

THE PROBLEM RESTATED

Nearly 40 percent of the public school students in the U.S. are African American, Latino, Asian, and Native American (NCES 2002, Table 42). Only 15 percent of teachers come from these groups (NCES 2002, Table 68). The discrepancies are even more dramatic in the central cities where Latino and African American youth have made up the majority of the student populations since 1981 (Schaerer, 1996).

Scholars have noted that the absence of non-white teachers deprives African American and Latino students of role models and creates a distortion of social reality for all children (Witty, 1982). A Los Angeles teacher, who is one of the few African American adults in her school, observes, "It's a good thing to have role models of the same ethnicity; it's very important. I know all the black students from kindergarten all the way up; there's just this automatic attraction. There are times when kids not even from my class stop and have conversations with me, whether it is a casual thing or they are having a problem." (Keleher et al., 1999)

The following equally significant problems are rarely noted:

1. The absence of African American and Latino teachers deprives many urban schoolchildren of the opportunity to have any permanent teacher. Teacher education has historically failed to staff urban schools or to accept responsibility for this failure (Haberman, 1986; Katz, 2004).

2. School teaching is a rapidly growing, stable job for college graduates. This job, one of the most widely available in many urban communities, is not available to half of the African American, Latino, and Asian college graduates who seek to enter it. Thus the parents of the most unemployed sections of the American population are deprived of one of the best jobs available in their communities—the job of teaching their own children and the children of their neighbors.

3. White teachers, widely acknowledged to be in need of multicultural training, are deprived of the very role models who might enable them to interact successfully with children from different cultures than their own (Goodwin, 1997; Ladson-Billings, 1991; Sleeter & Grant, 1994). Teacher education, as it is currently conducted, tends to reinforce rather than to challenge the racial-deficit models of white teachers (Yeo, 1997).

THE CAUSES RE-EXAMINED

In this chapter I will argue 1) that a major factor in urban school ineffectiveness and sometimes chaos is a set of state and federal laws which prevent urban schools from hiring those adult college graduates who have proven effectiveness working with students in urban schools; 2) that the lack of urban school teachers in general and "minority" teachers in particular is erroneously understood as a recruitment problem; 3) that the real causes rest on a racially skewed set of criteria for the initial selection of teachers; 4) that the selection system has its roots in white American racism, both institutional and ideological; 5) that the erection of an equitable teacher selection system will require struggle by those adversely affected by the present system; 6) that an equitable and educationally effective system would select candidates first on the basis of effectiveness in the classroom and would then require each to add to his or her knowledge base those elements missing in his or her undergraduate education; 7) and the attempt by Oakland's post-Civil Rights era school boards to create such a system reflected their equity orientation.

IS THE PROBLEM RECRUITMENT?

The absence of non-white teachers is generally regarded as a recruitment problem resulting from greater opportunities available to non-whites in other fields or to the lack of status which greets urban school teachers (Darling-Hammond, 1984; Cartledge, & Gardner, & Tillman 1995; Gordon, 1997; Shaw, 1996).

It is certainly true that non-white college graduates can often choose jobs other than teaching. However, it is also true that thousands of these college graduates do choose teaching and are unable to enter the field. The passing rates on the California Basic Educational Skills Test (CBEST) are just one indication of this reality. Most people who take this test have a college degree and sufficient interest in teaching to pay a $40 fee. However, nearly half of the non-whites who take it do not pass. So, half of the "recruits" become ineligible at the first gate. From July 1995 through June 1999, 228,738 people took the test in California. Their first-time pass rates follow: white (non-Hispanic) (81%), Asian American (68.7%), Mexican American (54.6%) and African American (42.4%). And the CBEST is only one, and perhaps the easiest hurdle facing new teaching recruits. Even those who support the CBEST as a reasonable requirement must acknowledge that it has a differential impact on college graduates by race, and the racial discrepancy in pass rates has not changed significantly over time.

SURVEYING THE IMPACT

A new era of teacher shortages and "higher standards" is making the situation worse. The U.S. Department of Education reports that 7 percent of public school teachers left the profession in 2001 and 8 percent moved to a different school (Luckers et al., 2004). Almost a third of new teachers leave teaching within the first three years (NCTAF, 2004). The percentage of people leaving teaching exceeded those entering the field by 23 percent, beginning in the 1990s (NCTAF, 2004). Teachers are not leaving primarily due to retirement. Three times as many people are leaving for other reasons. The National Council on Teaching and America's Future says a third of teachers are in flux each year, either entering or leaving the profession. Martin Haberman points out that teacher education has never prepared sufficient numbers of teachers for urban schools, throughout the life of the nation (Haberman, 1986).

I recently conducted a survey of four low-income middle schools in one school district about their staffing needs. Two months after the opening of school, one school had six teacher vacancies; one had seven; and two had three vacancies each. Another typical San Francisco Bay Area junior high school had seven classrooms staffed by a rotation of day-to-day substitutes throughout the last school year. This meant that approximately 800 children lived through educational chaos at least one hour per day for an entire year.

These are just a few of the dozens of such situations which I encounter every year, and the teacher shortage in Los Angeles and other cities is even more severe.

If you remember your own teachers as people who graduated from college and took a few credential courses, you will be interested to note the greatly expanded requirements which confront today's teacher aspirant.

California's teacher selection process is illustrative of the maze which confronts prospective teachers.

1. The prospective teacher must graduate from high school, an increasingly difficult endeavor for urban students in districts who face teacher shortages, violence, new high school graduation exams, and high dropout rates.

2. The prospective teacher must enter and graduate from college, another increasingly difficult chore in an era of increasing requirements, decreasing financial assistance, and more attacks on affirmative action.

3. Unless the individual clearly intends to teach when he/she enters college, he will not be told about the undergraduate prerequisites for entering a credential program. Thus, many teacher applicants discover at

graduation that they need additional coursework before they can enter a credential program.

4. All teachers must pass the California Basic Educational Skills Test (CBEST), which stops half of the non-white college grads who take it.

5. Programs which combine the credential preparation with a master's degree generally require the Graduate Record Exam, another standardized test on which more affluent individuals generally score better.

6. All elementary teachers and most secondary teachers must also pass a set of subject matter tests, California Subject Examinations for Teachers (CSET), each costing $150 or more, each lasting five hours, and each excluding an additional large percentage of Asian, Latino, and African American teachers.

7. Next the individual must find his way through a maze of interviews, coursework, and bureaucratic details administered by a college professoriate which is 86 percent monolingual white (NCES 2002, Table 228).

8. Then the individual must generally be able and willing to work for free for a year as a student teacher, a requirement which is virtually impossible for individuals with no accumulated family wealth. The accumulated net assets of the median white family are between five and eight times those of the median African American family (Conley, 1999). A year without income is an enormous burden for anyone, but the wealth gap means that it is often more possible for white than for non-white teacher candidates.

9. Recently, the implementation of No Child Left Behind has further complicated the situation by adding another layer of requirements to those already established by

the states. So, for example, college students who were promised that a "liberal studies program of study" in California colleges would meet the subject matter credential requirements, have now been told that because of No Child Left Behind, their lengthy subject matter preparation does not count, and they are required to take the standardized test which that coursework was supposed to replace.

10. The prospective teacher must complete over a year of post-B.A. coursework in teacher education.

11. The elementary teacher must pass an additional standardized test, the Reading Instruction Competence Assessment (RICA), and an additional Math Instruction Competence Assessment may be on the way.

Although politicians make an argument for the necessity of each of these steps, their total impact greatly skews the composition of the teaching corps in favor of whites.

Furthermore, this procedure does not select for ability in the classroom, because prospective teachers are not required to teach anything to anyone until they have completed most of this process and entered student teaching. At that point both the candidate and the institution are so invested in their preparation that few candidates are eliminated, even if they have not proven to be effective in the classroom (McKibbin, 2001).

THE VIEW FROM OTHER STATES

California has an extremely complicated and cumbersome set of requirements with multiple standardized tests and little flexibility, but the ethnic composition of teachers is little different in other states. The Southern Regional Education Board represents sixteen Southern states including

Georgia, Alabama, North Carolina, and Texas. The title of their report, "Spinning Our Wheels," tells most of the story. In some states the percentage of non-white teachers has declined in absolute terms; in no state has the percentage of African American and Latino teachers increased as rapidly as the percentage of students. In Arkansas the percentage of "minority" teachers decreased from 14 percent to 13 percent, while the percentage of "minority" students increased from 25 percent to 28 percent, and in Louisiana minority students increased from 43 percent to 51 percent while minority teachers decreased from 32% percent to 28 percent (SREB, 2003).

DIFFERENT TEACHER SELECTION PROCESSES FOR DIFFERENT SOCIAL CLASSES

The selection procedure I have described results in a several-tiered, class-based teacher selection system.

Wealthy private schools, unhampered by credentialing laws, hire those college graduates who exhibit a passionate interest in their subject matter and the willingness to spend endless out-of-class hours nurturing their affluent students both academically and socially, whether or not they possess a credential. I interviewed twenty teachers at elite private schools. A teacher at a school in Pebble Beach, California, told me that neither she nor most of her colleagues had teaching credentials. Both they and their employers considered the credentials irrelevant. A teacher at a New England private school explained that he did not meet many credential requirements but that he was highly valued at his school because he loved English literature, lived in the dormitories with the students, and provided countless hours of midnight tutoring and counseling.

Suburban schools which serve "middle class" children recruit, select, and tenure from the traditional credentialing system, and compete to find the limited number of teachers who can demonstrate the conformity to undergo the rigors of an irrational certification system and are at the same time good communicators and nurturers. Many teachers will choose these schools for two reasons: 1) these schools are often in communities like the ones where they live and grew up; 2) because all standardized test scores correlate strongly with family wealth, they are spared the endless reproaches and punishments which go with teaching a low-wealth student population who have the low scores that correlate with their family's low wealth levels.

Schools serving poor children are both strangled and condemned as they attempt to hire teachers. They are not allowed to hire the urban equivalent of the private school teacher—someone passionately committed and competent in teaching bilingual, non-white, non-affluent students. Yet they cannot find enough people with credentials to fill the schools, and many of those they do find flee after a month or a year, because they are either afraid of the students or unprepared for the demands of the job.

THE WHITENING OF THE TEACHING FORCE
AS PART OF AMERICA'S HISTORY
OF INSTITUTIONAL RACISM

No standardized test exists which produces equal results for members of all ethnicities and both genders (Persell, 1979; Sack, 2002). The decision to use a standardized test as an absolute gate for credential-seekers is thereby automatically a decision to exclude more members of non-anglo groups. Policy makers are fully aware of this impact when they decide to use a standardized test. Yet approximately forty-three states now use such tests with the result that half of the non-white college graduates who seek to become teachers are stopped at the gate by tests which have no demonstrated relationship to "teacher competency."

W.E.B. Du Bois predicted the institutional decisions which would lead to the elimination of African American teachers in a remarkable speech made scarcely one year after the *Brown v. Board of Education* desegregation decision. "The best of the Negro teachers will largely go because they will not and cannot teach what many white folks will long want taught." (Du Bois, 1954)

At the time of Du Bois' speech, approximately 82,000 African American teachers were responsible for the education of the nation's two million African American public school students. A decade later, over 38,000 black teachers and administrators had lost their positions in seventeen Southern and border states (Wilson, 1984).

The leading cause was the development of "teacher competency" testing, a practice which some have suggested had its roots in the desire of white Southern school systems to prevent black teachers from joining the newly integrated systems attended by Southern white children (Haney, 1987).

Those African Americans weeded out by the new credentialing laws have been extolled by highly educated African American; adults who attended segregated schools (hooks, 1994), their effectiveness is further indicated by the rapid rise in literacy among African Americans who attended these schools in the period from 1900 through 1950 (Anderson, 1995).

WHITE RACISM AND THE COMPOSITION OF THE TEACHING FORCE

Throughout U.S. history a series of laws have enforced the predominance of whites in countless economic arenas. In each case the law was presented by its advocates as the most rational approach to the situation at hand. These laws have included legalized slavery of Africans; legalized exclusion of Chinese from schools (Almaguer, 1994); legalized confiscation of the land of Mexicans and Indians; poll taxes and tests which excluded African Americans from voting; and the legalized reservation of higher paying jobs for whites.

Newspaper columnist Beatriz Hernandez identified the teacher selection system as a case of institutional racism in a 1992 column on the CBEST exam. She noted that California allows monolingual English speakers to become Bilingual Teachers in Training, and that they are not required to pass exams in Spanish or in teaching methods for five years.

"Why can't Latinos get a teaching job while studying for the CBEST? Why can't they get their classes paid for? The monolingual teachers can. Why can't they get a temporary certificate?

"I hate to think of why. Some say it's racism."

The various financial and standardized test requirements operate in essence as a job reservation and segregation system for whites. The number of credentialed non-white teachers are so few that suburban school systems are under little real pressure to integrate their teaching faculties. Whites who choose teaching are assured of a plentiful supply of openings, including enough openings for college graduates who do not wish to be teachers but who use urban teaching as a two year temporary job to pay off student loans.

Advocates of the current credentialing system argue that each of the requirements is important for teachers, but that the test and grade point average requirements are basic prerequisites. I am arguing that it is a racially skewed world view which sees performance on norm-referenced, multiple-choice, English-only standardized tests to be a more important prerequisite than classroom management, bilingualism, or comfort and effectiveness working with urban and rural parents.

THE COUNTERARGUMENT

The most compelling response to the argument made in this chapter is the assertion that urban, low-income children will be further disenfranchised by having teachers who are not sufficiently knowledgeable in academic subjects, and that the tests, though racially biased, do measure a certain amount of academic knowledge. My answer is fourfold:

First, the knowledge and skills actually needed by any individual teacher far exceed those possessed by anyone entering a classroom for the first time. When I became a fully credentialed junior high school English teacher, I was a good writer and a creative lesson planner, but I knew little world literature and I did not possess the stage presence to keep thirty twelve-year-olds focused on my instruction. My neighbor, Mr. Markos, had great stage presence and much knowledge, but he called the Asian students "rice eaters." My other neighbor, Ms. Miller, had stage presence, knew world literature, and did not call the students racist names, but she was an African American woman who had been tracked out of academic math all her life and was therefore constantly threatened by being unable to pass the standardized tests. I needed knowledge and stage presence, Mr. Markos needed to be fired or retrained in cultural competence, and Ms. Miller needed math training. But Ms. Miller's lack of math knowledge was a less serious weakness for an English teacher than the weaknesses of either myself or Mr. Markos. Yet she was the person most likely to lose her job.

Second, after studying the question of whether current teacher tests are being used in such a way as to differentiate among candidates more on the basis of race than on the basis of teacher competence, Haney, Madaus, and Kreitzer state unequivocally that "current teacher tests, and the manner in which cut-scores are being set on them, are differentiating among candidates far more strongly on the basis of race than they are on the basis of teacher quality."(1987)

In addition, if the purported concern that the teachers of urban students should have basic skills results in the students having no teachers at all, it is surely counter-productive, since the only available tests select for race more than for competence and contribute to urban students having no teachers.

Finally, each teacher, no matter what his or her background, needs to engage in a constant, monitored process of growth and development, adding either those basic courses which were eliminated from his early education by a racially skewed tracking system (Oakes, 1985) or those courses which will add stage presence, racial sensitivity, technological understanding, parent organizing skills, advanced knowledge in world history, techniques to incorporate music, an understanding of the Socratic method, chaos theory, modern social theory, or any of a thousand other pieces of knowledge and skill helpful in nurturing the young minds entrusted to his care.

UNWORKABLE SOLUTIONS

The National Council for Teaching and America's Future has proposed "improving school conditions" as a major aspect of teacher retention. I certainly support this effort, and in some cases it has been done with good effect. However, "improving conditions" is a more complicated problem than it appears, because rapid teacher turnover is one of the causes of those very conditions. A school which is staffed with many day-to-day substitutes is likely to be chaotic. The principal may be so overwhelmed with handling the issues which arise from the chaos that the teacher support and atmosphere management which would lead to "good conditions" become quite difficult. Missing textbooks, vandalism, student morale, and parent satisfaction all relate to the time wasted by students, especially in secondary schools, when they do not have permanent teachers, and these factors translate into more teacher loss.

Teach for America is also cited by some as a solution to this problem, but its actual effect is very questionable. I have known a number of Teach for America recruits who loved teaching, performed well, and chose to stay in urban classrooms. Any critique of the program must acknowledge this reality. But the majority come from non-urban schools (often elite Ivy League schools) and are therefore generally unfamiliar with urban students when they begin Teach for America. During their two-year commitment, which is advertised as a form of community service, they earn a full teacher's salary, receive loan repayment on undergraduate student loans, receive extra stipends through Americorps and summer preparation programs, and generally move out of the profession after two years, just when they have enough experience to make potentially competent teachers.

BETTER SOLUTIONS

Among the most successful solutions enacted over the past fifteen years is the use of something called "alternative certification." These programs begin by solving the most critical problem faced by people who do not possess the accumulated wealth needed to work for a year without pay. Under these programs, teachers complete their preparation while working for a teacher's salary. Teachers prepared in alternative programs are 46 percent people of color, which is twice the percentage of those prepared in California's traditional programs (McKibbin, 2001). Those prepared through alternative certification are also more likely to take jobs in "hard to staff" schools (usually low-income) and retention statistics are much higher. "As a condition of grant renewal, Teaching Internship Grant Programs are required to provide retention information for each cohort of interns. Recently the grant programs provided data for the last five cohorts, which include more than 10,000 interns. Of those that have been teaching one year 98 percent have been retained; two years 93 percent; three years 91 percent; four years 85 percent; and five years 77 percent are still teaching." (McKibbin, 2001) Other studies have found that those prepared in alternative certification are equally successful in the measures held most dear by government officials, the standardized test scores of their students.

SYSTEMIC SOLUTIONS: RACISM AND RESISTANCE

American racism is reduced when it is resisted. Slavery was only ended by the Civil War. Legal segregation yielded only to a massive Civil Rights movement. Understanding that the composition of the teaching force is a case of institutional racism, rather than a problem of recruitment, is critical to formulating an effective response. Recruiting individual non-whites to jump over the hurdles of the credentialing process (Cartledge et al., 1995) cannot provide enough teachers to end the massive urban school teacher shortage.

We need organized resistance to the exclusionary credential laws. An effective national campaign would require a coalition of civil rights and education organizations to oppose credentialing regulations which disproportionately exclude non-white college graduates and insist that such measures be compensated by other measures which mitigate their impact.

EXAMPLES OF SUCCESSFUL RESISTANCE

Several efforts have taken up explicitly the racial bias aspect of the credentialing process. The public interest law firm Public Advocates brought suit on behalf of 40,000 African American, Latino, and Asian educators who had been denied employment in California public schools since the CBEST was implemented in 1982.

The suit was filed in 1992 by attorney John Affeldt, on behalf of the 1,700 members of the Alliance of Mexican American Educators, the 300 members of the California Association for Asian-Pacific Bilingual Education, and 11 individual teachers. The U.S. Equal Employment Opportunities Commission had found the test discriminatory in 1990 but did not sue the state.

Supporters of the test said that it was created to ensure that prospective teachers possess basic skills. But plaintiffs in the Public Advocates suit argued that the primary form of teacher incompetence is the inability of teachers to translate their knowledge into learning for their students, and that the state has no effective way of dealing with this issue, while it already possesses multiple measures of basic skills including the requirement for five years of college and additional teacher tests, including the Multiple Subjects Aptitude Test and the Single Subject Aptitude Test.

In addition, the setting of the passing score on these tests is arbitrary but critical to the fate of non-white teachers. Were the passing score set one or two points lower, thousands of additional Latinos, African American, and

Asian teachers would be allowed to teach. Yet there is no particular "scientific" reason" for deciding that 29 points or 31 points or 33 points are sufficient to pass a particular section (Berlak, 1999).

The plaintiffs did not win the suit, the nation's largest ever employment discrimination lawsuit. However, the California Commission on Teacher Credentialing was forced to make a number of changes in the test in order to defend it in court. The most significant change was allowing individuals extended time in retaking a particular section of the test. I have personally spoken with fifty or sixty individuals who were positively affected by this change alone. Elena H., for example, earned passing scores on her last re-take, because the extended time compensated for the fact that English is her second language.

A second example is the Oakland Partnership Program, one of the first and most successful of the programs created under the alternative certification law described above. Details of this program are discussed in the following chapter.

CREATING AN ATMOSPHERE OF SHARED STRUGGLE AND ACHIEVEMENT IN URBAN SCHOOLS

A person's color does not ensure her success with any particular group of children. But one has only to read bell hooks's account of her early education to recognize the potential educational power of a school in which the expectations and ethos of community-connected adults prevail upon the consciousness of children.

"Almost all our teachers at Booker T. Washington were black women. They were committed to nurturing intellect so that we could become scholars, thinkers, and cultural workers—black folk who could use our 'minds.' We learned early that our devotion to learning, to a life of the mind, was a counter-hegemonic act, a fundamental way to resist every strategy of white racist colonization."(hooks, 1994)

It would take more than hiring a few more African American teachers to create the atmosphere of shared struggle and achievement which hooks describes in a modern urban school system. But were black and Latino and Asian adults to achieve true "empowerment" within schools a new form of culturally relevant and rigorous education might result.

7

Turning Lemons into Lemonade

The Partnership Program

OAKLAND AND MANY OTHER URBAN districts found themselves without enough teachers for reasons described in the last chapter. The districts' only recourse was to employ college graduates who were effective with students but had not yet achieved credentialed status. These individuals were often hired using something called "emergency permits." One newspaper report after another criticized urban districts for the use of "uncredentialed" teachers, but few of the reports explained the bureaucracy or the testing, and free student teaching requirements which contributed to this situation. Nor did they discuss the impossibility of staffing the schools without the use of "emergency permit" holders.

One aspect of the shortage and the short-term tenure of many teachers was the ethnic composition of available teachers. As explained in the last chapter, teachers who came from black, Latino, and Asian communities were more likely to stay in those communities and in teaching, because those were the communities where they lived and their skills and knowledge, such as second language knowledge, more closely matched the needs of those schools. So in the 1990s, 81 percent of California teachers and 46 percent of California students were white. The newly integrated Oakland school board made a commitment to address this problem. In 1991 then school board chair Toni Cook, at the request of civil rights activist and teacher educator Fred Ellis and a group of potential new African American and Latino teachers, directed that an effort be made to locate funding so that they could complete a credential program while working within the Oakland schools. As an outgrowth of that effort Ellis, personnel director Joe Taylor, and Marcus Foster Foundation leader Ada Cole pursued funding for a program which ultimately became a partnership between California State University Hayward and the Oakland school district.

Ellis had graduated from Morehouse College and participated in the southern Civil Rights movement. He was not afraid to address the racial causes of urban school problems. He believed that he could find hundreds of Latino, Asian, and African American college graduates who would want to teach in Oakland, but he would need to help them overcome a series of practical problems. He developed a three-pronged approach which aimed to address the major barriers: 1) help new teachers maintain a paid job while working on the credential, in order to eliminate the impossible requirement of working for free as a student teacher. Many of the potential teachers already had a paid teaching job under the "emergency permit" provision. Ellis's program would help those who were effective teachers to move from this status to full credentials. 2) create a recruitment, instruction, and support system run primarily by African American, Latino, and Asian educators which emphasized the community service aspect of teaching and helped prospective teachers confront the many financial and personal problems facing people of color, and 3) help with test fees and test preparation through nurturing assistance specifically personalized for candidates of color.

Ellis was concerned about discriminatory testing, but he argued that this was not the biggest barrier. "It is money, mostly money, that keeps black people out of teaching. If there is a real job, they will find a way around the other problems."

At the time of its creation the Partnership Program was completely unique. First, the teachers, many of them "emergency permit" holders, were able to finish their credentials while working. Previously these teachers could never finish their credentials because they could not do the required free student teaching, and the credential courses they needed were offered during the day when they were teaching classes in the schools. So after a few years of teaching most would leave the profession and further contribute to the disruptive teacher turnover which plagued urban schools for decades. Ellis's program allowed these teachers to remain in their classrooms as "interns" who would take classes in the evening and possess full credentials at the end of two years. The program was different in other ways. The faculty teaching the courses were far more diverse than the typical teacher education faculty, and more than half were themselves successful urban teachers. The courses were held on-site in the Oakland schools rather than twenty miles away in a distant college classroom.

The proposal to fund the project described other innovations, including the idea that the program would assume a different knowledge base for successful teaching. "In addition to the work of educational psychologists, historians, curriculum experts, and assessment specialists, new teachers need to 'know' the community. They must know, among other things, the thinking of children, parents, and community leaders; the changing sociopolitics of the district; the resources available to solve problems; the changing demographics and the immigration history of various groups." And it "acknowledged parents, grandparents, community organizations, churches and the entire Oakland community as partners in the preparation of effective teachers." (Kensington, 1995, pp. 6–7)

The other outstanding difference was the amount and type of support provided to teachers. From the moment Ellis and his colleagues concluded that an applicant would make a good Oakland teacher, the person was provided every form of consideration. Ellis's assistant, Brenda Mapp, provided endless hours of tutoring for those attempting to pass various tests. Ellis was available at home in the evening to talk by phone with nervous or confused applicants. The extra aspects of this support were funded by a grant for "alternative certification" which in subsequent years became a program in other California schools. Now many districts have alternative certification programs, although few are as personal, as innovative, and as successfully diverse as the Oakland Partnership was in the five years under Ellis's leadership.

In fact, Oakland is credited with having the most diverse teacher pool in the state, and large responsibility for this accomplishment has been attributed to the Partnership Program (Keleher et al., 1999).

THE EXPERIENCE OF THE NEW TEACHERS

A curator turned art teacher says his year in the Partnership Program was the "best year of education of my life." He is generally critical of teacher education and says he sees those "twenty-three-year-olds trained in other programs cracking up in the classroom."

The graduates of the Partnership Program are a remarkable group, having assumed leadership in dozens of institutions, some within the traditional education system, some outside of it, and some in opposition to it.

Candidates in the 1997 cohort provide some interesting examples. Nine of them were recommended for awards to the Seventh Annual Conference of the National Association for Alternative Educator Preparation Certification and Licensure. Their subsequent achievements are noteworthy. Two of the nine became principals; one became a lead teacher and acting principal; one is a highly esteemed elementary teacher in West Oakland and a union activist; one held together the atmosphere for a school in East Oakland for several years and is now the only African American male math teacher in a nearby suburban high school, and one was recently featured in the National Education Association's January 2005 issue as the leading teacher in the best of Oakland's "new small high schools." One left the area for graduate school and one left teaching. Eighty-seven percent stayed in teaching; of these all stayed in urban schools. Five are African American, one is Latino, one is Asian, and two are white.

One of the nine grew up in West Oakland in the same neighborhood described by Norma in chapter 2 of this book. Says Brenda Mapp, who worked part-time for the Partnership Program and is now a lead teacher at an East Oakland elementary school:

> My commitment to teaching began informally as a child when I held classes on my front steps with as few as one or as many as six neighborhood children. Whatever I learned from a book, my mother, or school, I was always eager to share it with whoever would become a captive audience. Since my urban teachers were positive and uplifting influences in my life, I decided early on that

I wanted to be just like them. They lived in my neighborhood, attended my church, and shopped where my family also shopped.

Brenda then surprised her family by majoring in business and becoming a high-tech professional instead of a teacher. Although she moved to the suburbs and earned a high salary, she says "I knew I would never be truly happy until I became a classroom teacher." However, she says, "as a single parent and a high tech professional I could not give up my job to pursue a credential in a program that required me to attend classes during the day and do student teaching without compensation." When she found out about the Partnership Program it seemed "too good to be true." She notes that she was able to work for a teacher's salary while attending classes at night, that the instructors were hand picked and committed to the spirit of the program, that the classes were held in Oakland near her home and school location, and that she received extensive advice and support from the program. Brenda concludes with the following comment. "The joint efforts between the 'Program' and the district have refined a product, me, that was developed long ago, but wasn't quite defect free. I now have product features and attributes that will help me prepare members for Workforce 2000."

I chose to report on the nine described above because accurate information is available on all of them. But the accomplishments of many other Partnership graduates are equally remarkable, particularly for a group which completed its credentials within the last six or seven years. Antonio Cediel became assistant superintendent of the Boston Schools while completing a doctorate at the Harvard School of Education two years after completing Ellis's Partnership Program. David Montes de Oca became one of the first Latino principals in Oakland and head of the highly successful Urban Promise Academy. Dennis Guikema became the principal of an Oakland charter school for students in the process of dropping out of traditional high schools. Keith Brown was recently elected to the Executive Board of the Oakland Education Association, the first African American man to serve in this capacity in many years. Felipe Macay is an assistant principal in another Bay Area district. Maureen Nixon-Holtan leads the much acclaimed Health Academy at Oakland Technical High School. Jerome Gourdine is assistant principal at a middle school in East Oakland. Kyla Johnson and Lauren Cherry are Oakland elementary principals. And on and on.

A REFORM PROGRAM FOR TEACHER EDUCATION

A movement to reform teacher education should have several parts:

1. States and districts which do not have alternative certification programs should create them immediately and use them to assist with changing the composition of the teaching force.

2. These programs should emulate the racially conscious and racially sensitive features developed in Ellis's program to confront the different life experiences of people of color going into teaching.

3. State legislatures should proclaim that having a multiracial, multilingual teaching force is a goal. Any proposed legislation or regulation should be accompanied by an "Equity Impact Report" outlining its likely impact on the ethnic composition of the teaching force.

4. Teaching applicants should submit a college degree from an accredited institution with coursework in the

subjects to be taught as the basic requirement to begin teacher education coursework and teaching jobs.

5. In addition to general credential work, all individuals should construct a specific contract to complete those courses and develop those skills for which they need further development. For example, an elementary teacher with few college composition courses might be asked to participate immediately in a National Writing Project program. An individual without a second language might be asked to work on developing this skill during a summer language program.

6. Parents, students, and teachers from diverse class and ethnic backgrounds should be involved in deciding the criteria for teaching.

7. Teacher educators should demonstrate their own ability to teach in a diverse urban or rural classroom.

8. All fees and procedures which have a racially disparate impact on candidates should be dropped.

8

"Are You Bilingual Like Me, Miss Johnson?"

Ebonics Revisited

RECENTLY, I ASKED A SEMINAR OF NEW Oakland teachers, "What were you thinking in 1996 and 1997 when Oakland's Ebonics resolution made national headlines?"

At the time, Oakland's groundbreaking resolution identifying Ebonics as the language of many African Americans was widely ridiculed. One young Caucasian teacher spoke up: "I was watching television in New York, and I thought the district wanted white teachers to learn to speak Black English." A number of other participants nodded their agreement and echoed some variation of her response.

Then a 28-year-old African American man offered a different perspective: "I was in Baltimore," he said. "Most of all, we were just excited that black people had the political power to do such a thing. We wondered how they were able to get something like that passed."

This young teacher's comment moves beyond pedagogy to the heart of the power and politics which are a major theme of this book. Linguistically and pedagogically, Ebonics (or Black English, or African American Vernacular English, as it is called by some) has been accepted by virtually all linguists and thousands of educators worldwide. But politically, Ebonics was the Willie Horton of the struggle over Oakland school governance. While the Oxford University bookstore in England was featuring a full window display on Ebonics with praise from such scholars as Stanford professor John Baugh, California politicians involved in the attempted takeover of the district continued to make jokes about the "Ebonics fiasco."

Linguists have acknowledged for years that the language patterns of many African Americans constitute either a language or a dialect, distinct from the language or dialect of academic English. The Linguistic Society of America, the largest linguistics organization in the world, passed a resolution in January 1997 saying in part, "The variety known as 'Ebonics,' 'African American Vernacular English' and 'Vernacular Black English' and by other names is systematic and rule-governed like all natural speech varieties. In fact, all human linguistic systems—spoken, signed, and written—are fundamentally regular. The systematic and expressive nature of the grammar and pronunciation patterns of the African-American vernacular has been established by numerous scientific studies over the past thirty years. Characterizations of Ebonics as 'slang,' 'mutant,' 'lazy,' 'defective,' 'ungrammatical' or 'broken English' are incorrect and demeaning." Since the differences are historic and regular, they are not "wrong" or "bad grammar." They are a grammar unto themselves, which seems "bad" within the context of the racial power dynamic of America.

On the other hand, American advertisers have often found the innovations of African language and style to be very profitable, and this has included use of the "high five," "right on," or a thousand other terms and phrases created outside "mainstream" America.

Recognizing that money and jobs are governed by non-Ebonics speakers, most African American parents want their children to be able to speak and write the language most likely to bring access to jobs and further education. Yet the "home" or first language for many African American children is Ebonics.

The story of Oakland's historic struggle around language policy for African American students has been told in several books, including the very interesting book by Perry and Delpit called *The Real Ebonics Debate.*

This chapter delves into only two dimensions of the struggle and its aftermath: the continuing significance of the Ebonics resolution as a civil rights victory, and the relationship of this victory to the racially constructed image that people in Oakland were incompetent to rule themselves.

Many Oakland teachers have embraced the strategies recommended in the school board's 1996 Ebonics resolution. One such teacher, Freda R., explains, "We should not be using the concept of wrongness. You can tell kindergartners, 'Repeat that for me in standard English.' The 'deficit' thought implies that our children are not capable intellectually."

Many children have also embraced the idea. Kyla Johnson, a former fourth-grade teacher at Parker Elementary School, now an administrator, says that her students regularly joke with her about being bilingual:

"'Are you bilingual like me?' they say. 'I speak Ebonics and English.'"

"The high school kids are even more aware," says Johnson, who ran an after-school cable TV program called "Homework Hotline." "We have big debates. Some of the high school students argue for switching back and forth between English and Ebonics in order to get the Algebra concepts across to their high school TV audience."

Outside Oakland the pedagogical impact has been widespread. A high school literacy specialist in Portland, Oregon, recommends that teachers learn the rules of their students' first languages, including Ebonics, in order to teach them how those rules differ from standard English. She uses the example of third-person singular in African American vernacular, which has no "s." So the speaker of Ebonics will use "He say" rather than "He says." This Portland specialist and former English teacher, Linda Christensen, says, "We talk about when you want to use standard English and when you use your home language. They generate the list themselves. They figure out that audience dictates the language you use. But they have to come to it. That works much better than for me to say, 'This is wrong.'" (Flannery & Jehlen, 2005, p. 30)

In Richmond, California, teachers were trained in the methods advocated in the Ebonics resolution, a program called Standard English Proficiency (SEP—the name of the methodology addressed by the "Ebonics resolution"), for ten years. Diana, a Richmond elementary school teacher, reported that the training was excellent and the results were outstanding. She saw significant differences in the writing of students when she used contrastive analysis, pointing out the variation between "standard" English and Ebonics. Teachers mourn the loss of this innovative program, which was only recently cut from the Richmond schools because of budget deficits.

Sulaiman Robinson, a social studies teacher at Castlemont High School in Oakland, quotes his own students as saying, "We speak Ebonics and English" when asked what languages they speak. When discussing the problems of Spanish-speaking Latino immigrants, African American students said, "We have a hard time, too, because we speak Ebonics." However, Mr. Robinson is able to use their familiarity with the concept of Ebonics to talk about their writing. He talks about code switching and instructs the students to decide which approach, "standard" English or Ebonics, they plan to use in a particular oral presentation or paper. In a survey of three classes at other Oakland high schools, all the African American students were aware of Ebonics; most stated that they spoke it and that it was only appropriate in certain situations.

So the aims of the resolution, supported by Oakland administrators and school board leaders, such as Toni Cook, were accomplished: Many African American youngsters became aware that their speech patterns were not defective but were ordered and historically based and could therefore be chosen for particular situations. Using the "proper" forms for a college essay or a job application became a matter of choosing between two ordered possibilities, rather than aiming to remember an infinite number of potential "errors." The rest of Americans became aware that some African Americans speak a language or dialect rather than simple "slang." And linguists universally acknowledged the rule-based stature of black language.

In exchange for this intellectual and policy-changing advance, those who promulgated the resolution received brickbats, not accolades. The esteemed liberal newspaper, the *New York Times*, ran an editorial in January 1997 by Brent Staples called "Last train from Oakland," which said that the Oakland school board deserved the scorn which was heaped upon it.

There were a few, mostly in the black press, who understood the issue immediately, even from afar. Writing in the *Amsterdam News*, Charles Barron recognized the issue of power embedded in the debate. "We must understand that standardizing English doesn't mean that it's better or proper. It means that people in power want to impose their language on the masses in order to maintain their control and dominance." He concluded his editorial with these words: "As a leadership scientist and social activist, I say, hurry up! Bring Ebonics to New York City so we can build self-esteem and self-confidence in our children as they learn standard English without degrading the African roots embedded within their speech." (Barron, 1997, p. 10)

In response to the Reverend Jesse Jackson's criticisms of the Ebonics adoption, Etta Hollins, the chair of the Department of Teaching and Learning at Washington State University, wrote in an open letter: "The fact that so many individuals with limited experience and no formal education related to the theoretical and methodological practices of schooling feel empowered to speak as authorities is profoundly troublesome. I wonder if these same individuals would take such liberties and act with the same disregard for professionals in such fields as medicine, law, or engineering." (Hollins, 1997, p. 8)

Jackson eventually retracted his criticism of Oakland, but the newspapers never apologized for their wildly false interpretations. How could the reporting of this issue be so inaccurate that even many African American leaders on the East Coast were unable to decipher the true intentions from the media reports?

Some have given belated advice to the media about how to avoid the misinterpretation and "do it better" next time. And some have said that, while they had the right idea, the Oakland board was guilty of bad public relations, "naivete," poor wording, and so on.

According to those closest to the story, however, even these sympathizers have missed the point. Says a white media consultant, Ken Epstein, who conferred with school district leaders at the time of the resolution, "It was a media race riot. The Superintendent and the person in charge of the Standard English Proficiency program sat down with representatives of all the major networks and newspapers, the day BEFORE the school board meeting at which the resolution passed. They explained in detail that there was no intention to teach Black English to either students or teachers, that the Standard English Proficiency program they were using had been adopted by the State several years earlier, and so on. When they came out of that two hour briefing, Oakland school personnel were positive that they had clearly explained every nuance and dispelled every distortion. Yet, the next day the press reported exactly the inaccurate information which the district had already corrected for them."

And much later, even after some journalists and academics had provided an accurate report of events, political use was still made of the distorted view. In the midst of the second attempted takeover of the district in 1999, Mayor Jerry Brown and others posed the Ebonics resolution as an example of educational incompetence and Brown said in an interview with writer Jamal Watson, "I still don't know what they are trying to say." (Wilder, 1999, p. A1)

Here Brown played to an issue unstated by those who advocated for Standard English Proficiency. The Oakland school board's resolution was, in fact, a rather conservative resolution aiming for a pedagogically sophisticated method of bringing students to "mainstream" English. Even that proved unacceptable to the racial mindset of America, because, as Charles Barron pointed out, it placed all dialects of English on an equal par, when the racial equation in America requires the assumed superiority of the dialect called "standard."

But Jerry Brown's assertion that he "still could not understand them" hinted of a theme not even raised by the courageous creators of Ebonics policy. This issue has been addressed by few but James Baldwin and may be even more frightening to white power.

"Negro speech is vivid largely because it is private. It is a kind of emotional shorthand—or sleight-of-hand—by means of which Negroes express, not only their relationship to each other, but their judgment of the white world. And, as the white world takes over this vocabulary—without the faintest notion of what it really means the vocabulary is forced to change. The same thing is true of Negro music, which has had to become more and more complex in order to continue to express any of the private or collective experience." (Baldwin, 1959)

The media race riot was not then primarily a product of Oakland's incompetence, in either education or public relations. The Ebonics resolution hit two racial nerves: the idea that all dialects are equal in origin and communicative potential and the lurking, unstated notion that the black dialect is evolving in its communicative power about a subject which is ignored in standard American dialect—the evolving nature of racial injustice.

9

Making a Way Out of No Way

The Struggle for Academic Quality

IN THIS BOOK I HAVE DISCUSSED THE multiple dimensions of education and pointed out that the strictly "academic" component of schooling is not its only aspect. Hiring, contracting, textbook production and sales, governance, media portrayals, school size, and structure all are important features of American education, each with its own history and political economy, each impacted by the American racial structure, and each the subject of frequent and intense struggle.

But the struggle over academic quality is the most visible schooling issue, and there are a number of difficult contradictions between various groups who see themselves as working toward educational justice and quality. In this chapter I will describe several situations where these contradictions come into play. Then I will discuss the law commonly called "No Child Left Behind." I will return to our theorists, and finally I will suggest approaches for individuals caught in these contradictions at their local schools.

The central problem is this: Schools have a positive function and a negative function for the average non-affluent urban student and his parents. Schools provide a service, because they are a place to obtain skills and knowledge; they also act as a social sorter, moving some students forward in society and holding some back, generally along racial and class lines. Most urban families need the service and are harmed by the sorting.

Education activists say they want "better quality" education (enhancing the service aspect) but there is no generally accepted measure of quality in the U.S. except the sort of standardized tests which were initiated by members of the Eugenics movement a hundred years ago (which enhance the sorting aspect). If we want equal outcomes, how do we measure them? If we accept standardized tests as the measure, then are we not trapped in a box which is partially of our own making, because in the name of "quality" we have accepted inequality and sorting?

ARE THE TESTS REALLY SO BAD?

The tests are generally "norm-referenced," meaning that 50 percent of those taking the test must be above average and 50 percent must be below average. So, before you know anything about the test, you know that half the students taking it must inevitably be seen as deficient. Every legislator who says he wants all the students in the country to read "at grade level" is either displaying enormous ignorance or expecting enormous ignorance from his audience, because the meaning of "at grade level" is at or above 50 percent of the students in that grade. We need little math knowledge to see that 100 percent of the people cannot be better than the top 50 percent, no matter what the test or how excellent the instruction which preceded it.

Every norm-referenced standardized test is required, by definition, to produce results which spread the test takers over 100 percentiles, with half above and half below the 50th percentile. Therefore, every question on the test is designed to "differentiate" in order to produce that spread. Any question which will be answered correctly by most of the people in a group is useless, since every question must serve the test's overall purpose, which is to separate people into groups. These groups are called "percentile"on some tests and "basic," "below basic," and "proficient" on other tests.

This differentiating purpose is the reason the questions on norm-referenced tests seem so odd and stilted—the double negative question, for example: "Which of the following is not one of the reasons for...blah...blah?" Making the question, as opposed to the answer, difficult to understand ensures that many people will get it wrong because they did not understand what was being asked. And this, of course, is a major reason why students who speak a second language or have slightly different culture-based language nuances miss two or three extra questions, which may move them from a "Proficient" category to an unacceptable category on a test.

This is not the only problem with the tests. By the age of 12 or 13, half the kids in the country have had six or seven experiences of being "below" par on a number of standardized tests. Remember, norm referencing *requires* that half the students be below the acceptable level, which is defined as around the 50th percentile. So, by the sixth or seventh grade, the enthusiasm of half the students to comprehend convoluted test questions is nonexistent. They do not expect to do well; they have never done well; and given the structure of the test, they (or some other students equaling half of those taking the test), will not do well again.

And finally, some of the questions have content which advantages particular groups of test takers. Although some questions have neutral content with regard to the race of the person taking the test, some questions advantage those who are more white or more affluent. The new California test, for example, asks four questions based on a document of directions for using a computer to plan a vacation trip involving air travel, hotels, and so on. Although increasing numbers of non-affluent teenagers have some access to computers, few will have had any knowledge, practice, or context for planning expensive foreign travel. This would not be so bad if there were also a few questions which, in contrast, gave an advantage to non-affluent people. A question with a few words in Spanish or an allusion to Luther Vandross would increase the comfort zone of a different group of youngsters. However, the only questions referring to black, Latino, or Asian culture are those involving information which has already "crossed over" into white American life.

It is not the case that no low-income student could figure out the answer to the travel question. But some questions are more comfortable and more accessible to some groups. On those questions, more white and more affluent students are likely to do better. And their correct responses on those few questions will move them into a higher bracket on a norm-referenced test.

Some education advocates respond with the argument that urban children really DO have fewer skills than their suburban counterparts, and if we throw out the tests, how can we hold the educational system accountable for providing any skills at all? They are right, of course. There are two parts to the educational gap in test scores between wealthy and non-wealthy children. On the one hand, less affluent students are actually provided with less information and skills. And, on the other hand, the tests do not measure the skills and knowledge which those youngsters do have. Furthermore, the constant psychological defeat imposed by years of receiving low scores on norm-referenced tests probably actually depresses the achievement of some youngsters over time. Every urban high school teacher has dozens of stories about tenth and eleventh graders who just "bubble in any answer." Those who react in horror to such student "irresponsibility" should remember that even a mouse in a cage will stop pushing the experimenter's lever if he is never rewarded with any cheese.

Among those seeking educational justice, some are willing to accept the tests in order to have a measure of student information acquisition, and some think this concession leads not to quality but to an even greater achievement gap as teachers and students are punished by the nature of the tests and their persistent correlation to greater family wealth.

EXAMPLES OF THIS CONTRADICTION IN REAL LIFE

Schools are both the source of valuable skills and the site of oppressive sorting and differentiating. How do we enhance the socially useful aspect and reject the sorting aspect? When I speak to groups of teachers, they say, "We have read about how the school system reproduces the social order. Then you tell us to be great teachers, to be enthusiastic, and to help our students get to college. It's an impossible contradiction!!"

A related contradiction arises when we examine the action of the civil-rights oriented school boards. In Chapter 5, I described two school board resolutions, one requiring algebra for all ninth graders and the other imposing grade-level textbooks for all classes, which were introduced by Oakland school board members in the 1980s. In both cases, many activists, especially teachers and curriculum specialists, considered the motions ridiculous.

NO CHILD LEFT BEHIND

It is within the context of the contradiction between the service aspect and the sorting aspect of schooling that the law commonly called "No Child Left Behind" was passed in January 2002. It has a number of painfully unfair provisions created on the basis of the flawed logic I have been describing throughout the book. It took the legitimate concern with the low test scores of poor students and turned this concern into a battering ram against the schools attended by those very students. The law specifically targets poor schools, because its provisions are tied to funding which comes from the federal government for "disadvantaged" students. Only a state such as Vermont, with its overwhelmingly white population, found it possible to reject the funds and all the strings that went with them. Teachers and administrators of poor districts scramble to meet the provisions of a law which blames them for the problems of their students.

As I have described throughout this book, that blame is wrongly placed. The law requires "highly qualified" teachers and ignores the fact that the necessary numbers of those considered "qualified" do not exist. The law requires 95 percent participation by all subgroups of students, ignoring the fact that by high school, 95 percent of the students do not come to school on any given day, let alone on test day. And their absence is often due to such practical issues as lack of bus fare or the need to provide occasional care for younger children while their parents go to work. The law requires that 100 percent of students meet "proficiency" by 2014. This provision, more than any other, makes clear that the authors never really believed the "goals" of the law would be met, because no group ever achieves 100 percent on any task, including getting up in the morning. The law requires *all* students to "meet proficiency," including those who have been in the country only for a short time. I would venture to guess that none of the legislators who voted for the law has become as academically proficient as a native speaker within two years of learning a foreign language. And, less often noted, but most pernicious, the law requires school districts to turn over contact information for all students to military recruiters unless the individual parent discovers this provision of the law and how to opt out of it.

The most feared provision of the law calls for major restructuring of individual schools based on not meeting the "adequate yearly progress" targets required by the law. For reasons discussed above, the targets are completely unrealistic for the poorest schools and the requirements tend to enhance rather than dispel the chaos in these schools. The "most qualified" teachers have an additional reason to leave these schools, because, even if they are committed to teaching poorer children, many are unwilling to stick around for the merciless scrutiny and unrelenting "test prep" programs which are generally seen as the route to "meeting the targets." The easiest way for any individual teacher to raise his or her test scores is to stop teaching in a poor school and go to work in a wealthier school. He will not need to teach any better. His students' scores will go up as an automatic result of the correlation between family wealth and test scores in American schools.

Nevertheless, those committed individuals who are unwilling to run away from urban schools are finding ways to struggle for justice within the provisions of the law. The law which requires school restructuring has several provisions for how this restructuring can be accomplished, including the possibility of turning the school over to a for-profit charter company. However, the fifth alternative in the restructuring requirement allows for "any other major restructuring." Activists in the West Contra Costa and Oakland school districts pursued two avenues in the attempt to turn this bad thing into a good thing. In West Contra Costa, members of the March4Education coalition of parents and teachers proposed greater authority for School Site Councils in making decisions at schools which are being "restructured." In Oakland, teachers and parents proposed that coalitions of parents, community organizations, and teachers become the governing body for each school. And there is now nationwide opposition to the law, including a lawsuit arguing that the law is not enforceable because the federal government is requiring actions on the part of states which are not supported by the required federal dollars.

CONTRADICTIONS BECOME OPPORTUNITIES

There is no immediate resolution to the dilemmas I have described. The economic system produces billionaires and paupers; the educational system is tied to it, and therefore overall justice will not occur as a result of any easy and immediate set of new policies proposed by either liberals or conservatives. However, perspective on how to operate in light of these contradictions is provided by our theorists Bell, Freire, Marx, and others. The critical race theorist, Derrick Bell, in discussing the need to struggle in spite of the permanence of racism, refers to a gospel song which asks, "What do you do when you've done all you can and it feels like it's never enough?" and answers, "Just stand." (Bell, 2004, p. 180) Bell refers to law professor Robert Gordon with his provocative resolution to the dilemma:

Things seem to change in history when people break out of their
accustomed ways of responding to domination, by acting as if the
constraints on their improving their lives were not real and that
they could change things; and sometimes they can, though not always in the way they had hoped or intended; but they never knew
they could change them at all until they tried. (Gordon, 1990)

Enrique Trueba talks about "pedagogical optimism,"
the belief that education can change the world (Trueba,
1998). And Paulo Freire reminds us that knowledge and
the educational system are not synonymous by urging us
to "read the word" and also to "read the world."

Ironically, Marx's detractors often speak of him as a
determinist. Yet, Marx was the most activist of any 19th
century scholar. When he was not studying political economy, he was traveling around Europe organizing workers
to oppose the dramatic impact of industrial capitalism on
their lives. As the certain father of what is now called "action research," Marx believed that we study the world in
order to change it, and his tombstone bears these words:
"The philosophers have only interpreted the world in
different ways, the point however is to change it." Thus,
while Marx's analysis led him to see the operation of the
economy as a function of system and history, rather than
a matter of individual human policies, at the same time he
believed that the intervention of masses of human beings
could change that systemic functioning. Furthermore,
Marx saw each new development in capitalism as an opportunity for its opponents to push forward movements
for social justice.

A literacy coach working in a Latino community in an
agricultural area of California recently commented on the
painful double-consciousness that comes from recognizing the big picture of unfairness, while continuing to tell
her students they can achieve great things. At the end of
several days of personal struggle with these issues, she said,

"I am friends with a lot of bilingual teachers whose parents worked in the fields. They have walked with and worked with Cesar Chavez. Interestingly enough—they seem to get less frustrated at times—I think they see the struggle as part of life and something natural and healthy to do."

Injustices within the educational system sometimes create a spot at which the system explodes and new opportunities open up. Southern segregation in the U.S. and South African apartheid are two important cases of this phenomenon. Schools were segregated in the South because of white racism, but the isolated communities which they produced became the location of widespread conversation and organizing about civil rights. And when the Civil Rights movement broke out, the segregated educational institutions of the South were among the strongest bases of support for its development.

No school system could have been more thoroughly "reproductive" of the broader political system than the apartheid education of Black South African youngsters. In this case, the imposition of new injustices, specifically the requirement that all education be conducted in the hated language of Afrikaans, led to new organizing and major marches, and was ultimately a factor in the complete dismantling of the apartheid system.

In summary, the educational system is unjust, but the ideas and the struggles which emerge within that system can provide the momentum for change in education and sometimes in the broader society.

INCREASING THE MOMENTUM

The next chapter will discuss broad-ranging policy struggles.

In the conclusion of this chapter I will argue for three actions close to home, in the classrooms and schools where local parents and teachers are attempting to "make a way out of no way."

First, teachers need models of teaching which are both critical and rigorous, both emancipatory and serious about academic skills. The best description for pedagogically hopeful and systemically critical classroom teaching is provided by Gloria Ladson-Billings in her wonderful article on Ms. Lewis in "The Liberatory Consequences of Literacy." Teachers who followed her platform could change the world.

Second, anything that personalizes a school is likely to improve our chances of transformative change, because it increases the possibility that parents, students, and teachers will know each other well and therefore have the chance for genuine and thoughtful alliances. There is a certain motion in the direction of smaller schools which equity minded individuals and coalitions should push forward.

Third, there is a missing link in the public critique of No Child Left Behind which has to do with a muted critique of testing. Liberal educators tend to oppose the tests for the following reasons: The tests are used to blame school problems on teachers. They trivialize the curriculum by focusing on minor pieces of information. They distort the curriculum by focusing only on those subjects which can be tested on paper and pencil tests. They are enormously expensive and this expense is paid to test-producing companies by taxpayers. This is money which could be used directly at school sites. The testing takes an enormous amount of time. The tests ignore widely accepted information about child development. The tests are unfair, because the resources available to various schools are not the same.

All of these arguments are true and important. However, they are insufficient to move urban parents to action. If the only problems are time and money, the parents will not engage in the sort of struggle which would be required to reduce the testing.

The two most important aspects of the tests are: 1) Because they are norm-referenced, they are essentially rigged. Although business-connected reformers pose the new tests as "standards-based," they continue the assumptions and practices of all norm-referenced tests. They eliminate all test questions which do not serve to differentiate among students, with the result of creating a normed curve (Haney, 2002 p. 2). They are racist, not on individual questions, but in overall conception and structure. Anti-testing advocates sometimes avoid the issue of race, because they want to maintain a coalition with white parents. This is an unworkable concession, because it deprives those most hurt by the tests of the information needed to oppose them. Among the most important (and also most difficult) victories we could win would be ending norm-referenced punitive tests and replacing them with an assessment system which was publicly created by ethnically, culturally, geographically diverse groups of people with the aim of appreciatively evaluating students' emerging competence and prescribing education to enhance it.

10

Conclusions and Programs

LEGAL SCHOLAR AND CRITICAL RACE theorist Derrick Bell describes two sorts of U.S. policies in regard to race. In the first, racial-sacrifice covenants, black rights are sacrificed for the interests of policy-making whites. In the second, interest-convergence policies, "Black rights are protected only in and so long as policy makers perceive that such advances will further the interests which are their (whites') primary concern." (Bell, 2004, p. 49)

This book describes many instances in which the African American school board majority was able to assert local black rights with less regard for interest convergence, because of the temporary strength of black political power in Oakland. The district began a program to increase the percentage of teachers of color, supported the Ebonics resolution, rejected the Houghton-Mifflin series, rejected tracking, changed the contracting process to include more minority firms and internal employees, rejected overtures from such profit-making firms as Edison Charters, eliminated tracking, and most important, maintained financial control of the school district. This is not to say that they directly or purposely confronted white constituents. For example, they did not dismantle several mostly white hill schools whose attendance was determined by residence. These small elementary schools were often more than 50 percent white, although the district as a whole was 90 percent children of color. Board members did not apparently consider that forcing the integration of these small schools would be of particular benefit to communities of color. Where issues did seem to hold potential benefit for students of color, however, they did not back down before their critics, which included white "progressives," publishers, contractors, attorneys, media figures, and others. Remarkably they were able to hold on to this power for fifteen years.

THE RETURN OF RACIAL SACRIFICE AND INTEREST CONVERGENCE

During the last year of their authority, they selected lifetime Oakland resident and career educator Carole Quan as superintendent, the first Asian American woman to lead a major district in the U.S. Although she held the position for only a year, she oversaw the first small increase in test scores to take place in many, many years. She and her predecessor, Carolyn Gettridge, initiated the first move toward smaller, personalized high schools using the only funding available at the time, the allocations for career academies. Carole Quan was extremely popular in the black community, because she regularly visited black churches and black events and expressed ongoing concern with the needs of

Oakland's black students, who were still the majority of students in the district at the time.

The attack on the power and policies of the black majority was essentially uninterrupted throughout their tenure, but the push to unseat them heated up again in 1999. Two factors were decisive in their ultimate defeat. First, they lost the leadership of Sylvester Hodges, when he retired from the school board. Hodges' vision was quite clear when it came to the machinations of white power, and he proved irreplaceable as a cohesive force. Second, politician Don Perata had been steadily building a new political machine in Oakland which was pro-developer, aligned with new mayor Jerry Brown, and essentially committed, like Brown, to the "dismantling of African American leadership." Perata introduced a bill in the state legislature in 1999 which would have removed the power of the elected board, not based on financial issues, because Hodges had kept the district budget carefully balanced, but based on something Perata called "academic bankruptcy." This description was based on the norm-referenced standardized tests which showed Oakland scoring low, just like every other district with poor children. The headlines were large, the accusations enormous, but the community rallied against the bill in the state capital, and Perata looked a bit foolish with his legislative colleagues. Perata ultimately agreed to withdraw the bill in exchange for the resignation of Carole Quan as superintendent. Quan resigned. With Perata's support, Dennis Chaconas was selected as the new superintendent. Chaconas was able to garner the support of white developers and foundations, which was never available to the African American oriented administration.

Chaconas himself was unseated only a couple of years after his accession to power. There seem to have been two major reasons. First, unlike the African American board majority which had preceded his tenure, Chaconas ignored the fact that financial solvency was key to maintaining control of the district. Second, he was perhaps not sufficiently compliant with the wishes of kingmaker Don Perata, who abandoned him and initiated a successful state takeover of the district in 2003 (Thompson, 2004; Gammon, 2003).

WHY DOESN'T OAKLAND HAVE GREAT SCHOOLS?

Oakland has a solid history of civil rights commitment—so why doesn't it have great schools throughout its system? The answers intersect with the major themes of critical race theory: the harmful fictions of colorblind liberalism, the web of rights afforded to whites because of their race, and the unwillingness to acknowledge racism as a factor in both the conditions and the policies surrounding urban school districts. The school board members had full-time jobs in fields outside education. They were obliged to hire administrators who had been trained in the same system they were attempting to uproot. To the extent that these administrators had any transformative and race-conscious vision, they battled in an arena consisting of vast state regulation, rotting buildings, seniority arrangements, and routine business and media assault. On one occasion when the board attempted to select a true race-conscious "outsider" as superintendent, the state superintendent of schools interfered immediately and harshly to prevent his hiring.

The second and related reason has to do with the extent to which state and federal regulation increased in direct proportion to the rise of more racially representative school boards. Teacher credentialing is one outstanding example. As noted in greater detail in chapter 6, many Oakland students simply have no teachers because the vastly expanded and costly credential requirements have left those who are willing and able to teach Oakland's poor, multilingual population unable to meet the complex and expensive requirements to do so.

The third reason has to do with the ongoing impact of corporate policy on creating a tightly tiered public education system (Persell, 1977; Tyack, 1974; Domhoff, 2001; Emery & Ohanian, 2004). What is the role of corporate America in education? A hundred years ago, using the new spirit of industry as its model, business pressed public education to become efficient and productive. These reformers argued that their testing and tracking systems would make the schools efficient so that they could educate the mass of American children, including immigrants and non-white Americans (Tyack, 1974).

Now a new set of business leaders (led by such groups as Business Roundtable), a new set of testing companies, a new set of academics, and a new set of administrators (many of them trained at the same elite universities) are again arguing that standards and testing reforms will bring quality, efficient education to poor urban children. Just as their predecessors did in the early 1900s, those spearheading reform today argue that their proposals are the only way to achieve the desirable goal of "leaving no child behind." (Apple, 2001; Domhoff, 2001; Emery & Ohanian, 2004)

Both the early period of school reform and the more recent period are understood best through the lens of critical race theory and its critique of "colorblind liberalism."

A PEOPLE'S PROGRAM FOR EDUCATIONAL CHANGE

A national movement for education as a civil right needs a program to challenge the assumptions and direction of both the Business Roundtable agenda and the more right-wing agenda of complete privatization. When thoroughly developed, a people's program could become the litmus test for supporting candidates for public office. Support by civil rights and education organizations could be provided only to those who took action on elements of the adopted program.

ON STRATEGY

1. A people's movement should resist close alliances with the business organizations whose first priority is short- and long-term profits. The Business Roundtable is eager to make alliances with unions and parent groups, because it wants to unite all significant organizations behind its program. And it frames its program in positive-sounding messages like "ending the achievement gap." In fact, however, the achievement gap will be widened by any program which disempowers urban communities, measures schooling by standardized tests, and increases profit-making involvement in education. A people's movement will probably agree with business on some issues. In the 1920s, business wanted to universalize basic education. That was good. Business also wanted to track and segregate immigrant and non-white students. So it supported racist testing and tracking. That was bad.

   Bill Gates supports smaller high schools. I agree with that. The Business Roundtable supports more and more testing. I do not agree with that. The inclination to do what business wants because we "need their money" is ill-founded. The "contribution" of business to education should be paying taxes on the enormous wealth it accumulates in this country. Those who use the public schools should make democratic decisions about what happens in them.

2. In order to have any power in educational change, we need to be in the streets. Battles for more equitable schools were won in the Civil Rights era, because people rallied, demonstrated, picketed, and voted, These protests won some limitations on testing, the addition of ethnic studies content, the expansion of black and Latino employment, teachers union rights, increased access to college, and other issues.

3. Education is potentially a unifying issue for all communities of color. A representative and high-quality teaching force, a nonbiased curriculum, equitable funding, and respect for language differences are just a few of the many areas where the interests of the Latino, African American, Native American, and Asian communities are either similar or identical. Education should be a pivotal issue for those who work to unite communities of color against white hegemony in economics and policy making.

ON A PEOPLE'S PROGRAM

Here is a beginning program of demands for making education a civil right:

1. Democracy

   a. Fully functioning, locally elected school boards in every school district. End "punish the victim" takeovers of urban school districts. If any district has an elected school board, then every district should have one.

   b. Transparent and lessened involvement by the Business Roundtable in educational decision making.

   c. Parental power and consideration at each site such as that which is accorded to parents in expensive private schools. This should begin with a translator, a tour, and a cup of coffee when a parent enrolls a child at a school and should include a real voice in curriculum and staff selection.

2. Joy

The current educational reform agenda does not mention the most important educational standard: A love of learning, a spirit of community, and a sense of joy in individual and collective accomplishments.

   a. Aim for joyful classrooms and schools filled with a love of learning and of young people.

   b. Small, intimate learning communities, so that all students are connected to adults who know them well. This can also lead to less intrusive school site law-enforcement.

   c. Small classes so that students can be "apprenticed into a community of learners." (Ladson-Billings, 1992)

3. Bilingualism for all. Immigrant students should have their home languages protected, respected, and shared with other students. Multilingualism is also fundamental to a more internationalist outlook for U.S. citizens.

4. A multiracial, highly skilled, and culturally competent teaching force which is ethnically representative of the national student population, now nearly 40 percent Latino, African American, Asian, and Native American. Preparation in cultural competence and interactive

teaching methods for all teachers. Massive funding for the preparation of teachers in mathematics and science and time off to learn the best methods for teaching those subjects.

5. Assessment Reform

    a. End profit-making, norm-referenced, "blackbox" testing. Use only transparent learning assessments developed by non-profit organizations with input from urban and rural administrators, teachers, and parents.

    b. Voluntary, nonpunitive parent/student evaluation of teachers. Teachers would solicit, read, and respond to anonymous student and parent evaluations of their teaching. These evaluations would not be tied to teacher employment or pay.

6. Teacher development of curriculum, learning expectations, and lesson models with input from parents and students. Schedule the school day so that teachers can create, practice, and publish model lessons in each subject area.

7. End the torture of small children. Return to age-appropriate instruction. Examine models from other countries which have higher literacy rates than the U.S. and do not ability-group, retain students in the same grade, or try to teach four-year-olds to read. Based on this age-appropriate instruction, end grade retention and excessive, racially biased special education placements.

8. Reasonable college preparatory and life preparatory curriculum for all students. Create teacher-led panels to determine what all students can reasonably be expected

to learn in high school, This should include academic knowledge, arts curriculum, parenting and community service skills, hands-on skills such as construction, and physical curriculum in dance, sports, and fitness. These and only these should be the college entrance requirements, and an adequate number of teachers should be provided for each subject, so that students from wealthier communities would not have extra advantages in college application. No subject should be a college requirement if there are insufficient numbers to teach it to all students.

9. Take the profit out of public education. No for-profit charters or other for-profit educational enterprises with the use of public funding.

10. Funding should be increased in proportion to the fact that this really is a "knowledge economy." Sharing humanity's vastly expanding knowledge base with all young people cannot be accomplished using the funding levels of the past. However, no concessions on democracy, assessment, and program should be made in order to obtain this funding.

References

A history of intervention. (2002, January 9). *Education Week.*

Almaguer, T. (1994). *Racial Fault Lines: The Historical Origins of White Supremacy in California.* Berkeley: University of California Press.

American Association of Colleges for Teacher Education (AACTE). (1987). Teaching Teachers: Facts and Figures. Washington, DC.

American Association of Colleges for Teacher Education. (1994). Teacher education pipeline III: Schools, colleges, and departments of education enrollments by race, ethnicity, and gender. Washington, DC, ED 369 780.

Anderson, J. (1995). Literacy and education in the African-American experience. In W. C. Gadsden and D. A. Wagner (Eds.) *Literacy among African-American Youth.* Cresskill, NJ: Hampton Press.

Anderson, K. (1999, Nov 28). The next big dialectic; [Op-Ed]. *New York Times.* p. 4.11.

Apple, M. (2001). *Educating the Right Way: Markets, Standards, God, and Inequality.* London, England; New York: RoutledgeFalmer.

Applied Research Center (ARC). (1999, August). *Creating Crisis: How California Teaching Policies Aggravate Racial Inequality in Public Schools.*

Arrow, K., Bowles, S., & Durlauf, S. (2000). *Meritocracy and Economic Inequality.* Princeton, NJ: Princeton University Press.

Bagwell, B. (1982). *Oakland: The Story of a City.* Oakland Heritage Alliance.

Balancing accountability and local control: State intervention for financial and academic stability. (2000). Los Angeles, CA: Reason Public Policy Institute.

Baldwin, J. (1959, March 29). Sermons and blues. *New York Times.*

Barron, C. (1997, Jan 11). Quick! Let's get hooked on Ebonics. New York Amsterdam/ *News*, p. 10.

Battle lines drawn on state control of Oakland schools. (1989, September 11). *Los Angeles Times*, p. 3.

Baugh, J. (2000). *Beyond Ebonics: Linguistic Pride and Racial Prejudice.* Oxford, England: Oxford University Press.

Bell, D. A. (1989). *And We Are Not Saved: The Elusive Quest for Racial Justice.* New York: Basic Books.

Bell, D. A. (1993). Remembrance of Racism Past: The Civil Rights Decline. In Hill & J. E. Jones (Eds.) *Race in America: The Struggle for Equality* (pp. 73–82). Madison: University of Wisconsin Press.

Bell, D. A. (2004). *Silent Covenants: Brown v. Board of Education and the Unfulfilled Hopes for Racial Reform.* Oxford: Oxford University Press.

Bensky, L. (1995, December 15). Who's left? *East Bay Express.* p. 1.

Berlak, H. (1999). *Adverse Impact: How CBEST Fails the People of California.* Oakland, CA: Applied Research Center.

Blake, E. J. (Ed.). *Greater Oakland 1912.* Oakland, CA: Pacific Publishers.

Bowles, S., & Gintis, H. (1977). *Schooling in Capitalist America.* New York: Basic Books.

Burbules, N., & Torres, C. A. (Eds.). (2000). *Globalization and Education: Critical Perspectives.* New York: Routledge.

Cartledge, G., Gardner, R., and Tillman, L. (1995). African Americans in higher education special education: Issues in recruitment and retention. *Teacher Education and Special Education*, 18, 166–178.

CBEST decision appealed. (1997, Spring). *Fair Test Examiner.*

Chambers, S. (2002, Winter). Urban education reform and minority political empowerment. *Political Science Quarterly*, 117(4), 643–665.

Chapman, P. D. (1989). *Schools as Sorters: Lewis Terman, Applied Psychology, and the Intelligence Testing Movement. 1890-1930.* New York: New York University Press.

City schools fall short in general funds. (1989, September 29). *The Montclarion*, p. 1.

Classroom Teacher Newsletter. (1969, October 3).

Close, S. (1970, April 1). Oakland 5 trial raised questions. *The Catholic Voice.* No. 47, Diocese of Oakland, p. 1.

Colvin, R. L. (1996, Feb. 5). Suit challenges basic skills test for teachers as biased. *Los Angeles Times*, p. 1.

Community uproar. (2002, February). *American Teacher.* Retrieved March 1, 2004 from http://www.aft.org/publications/american_teacher/feb02/community.html

Conley, D. (1999). *Being Black; Living in the Red.* Berkeley: University of California Press.

Cookson, P., & Persell, C. H. (1989). *Preparing for Power: America's Elite Boarding Schools.* New York: Basic Books.

Cooper, C. C. (1986). Strategies to assure certification and retention of black teachers. *Journal of Negro Education*, 55 (1), 46–55.

Council for the Great City Schools. (1996). The Urban Teacher Challenge: A Report on Teacher Recruitment and Demand in Selected Great City Schools. Washington, DC: Council for the Great City Schools.

Cubberly, E. P. (1916). *Public School Administration.* Boston: Houghton Mifflin, p. 338.

Cutler, J. (1992, February 22). Groups say teacher test is unfair, *Oakland Tribune*, p. B-1.

Darling-Hammond, L. (1984). Beyond the commission reports: The coming crisis in teaching. Santa Monica, CA: Rand Corporation. ED 248 245.

Dee, T. S. (2004, Febuary). Teachers, race, and student achievement in a randomized experiment. *The Review of Economics and Statistics*, 86 (1), 195.

Delpit, L. (1996). *Other People's Children: Cultural Conflict in the Classroom*. New York: New Press.

Directory of the Oakland Public Schools 1936–37; November 1935, Office of the Administration Building, 1025 2nd Avenue

Domhoff, W. (2001). *Who Rules America: Power and Politics*. 4ᵗʰ edition. New York: McGraw Hill.

DuBois, W. E. B. (1970). Two hundred years of segregated schools. In P. Foner (Ed.), *W. E. B. DuBois Speaks: Speeches and Addresses, 1920–1963*. New York: Pathfinder.

Education Commission of the States. (2001). *Policy Brief: State Takeovers and Reconstitutions*. Denver, CO: ECS.

Edwards, T. B., Project Director, *McClymond*. (1968). *A Problem in Urban Renewal*. University of California, Berkeley.

Elliott, John E. (1987). Moral and ethical consideration in Karl Marx's robust vision of the future society. *International Journal of Social Economics* 14(10), 3, 24.

Emery, K. & Ohanian, S. (2004). *Why Is Corporate America Bashing Our Public?* Portsmouth, NH: Heinemann.

Epstein, K. K., & Ellis, W. F. (1992, April). Oakland moves to create its own multicultural curriculum. *Phi Delta Kappan*.

Epstein, K. K., & Ellis, W. F. (1992, October). Getting the story straight. *Phi Delta Kappan*.

Epstein, K. K. (1992, November). A test that rules out good teachers. *San Francisco Examiner*.

Epstein, K. K. (1993). Case studies in dropping out and dropping back in. *Journal of Education*, 174 (3), 55–65.

Epstein, K. K. (1993). Toward a representative teaching force. *Kappa Delta Pi Record*, 29 (4), 128.

Epstein, K. K. (1996, January 9). A test that's costing us real teachers. *Los Angeles Times*.

Epstein, K. K. (1997, October 10). Education poses tricky questions. *San Francisco Chronicle*.

Epstein, K. K. (1997, December 10). Tests and naked emperors. *Oakland Tribune*.

Epstein, K. K. (2000, February 13). It's all about politics, Not Oakland's students. *San Francisco Chronicle.*

Epstein, K. K. (2003). Disenfranchising black voters: California style. *Oakland Post.*

Epstein, K. K. (2004, June). Miracle school: Child of the civil rights movement. *Phi Delta Kappan.*

Flannery, M. F., & Jehlen, A. (2005, January). Closing the gap. *NEA Today*, pp. 22–33.

Foster, M. (1990). The politics of race: Through the eyes of African-American teachers. *Journal of Education*, 172(3), 135–141.

Freire, P. (1970). *Pedagogy of the Oppressed.* New York, NY: Continuum.

Freire, P. (1994). *Pedagogy of Hope.* New York: Continuum.

Gammon, R. (2003, August 18). Phone logs link 'politics' to school takeover. *Oakland Tribune*, p. 1.

Gammon, R. (2004, January 5). School spending challenged. *Oakland Tribune*, p. 1.

Gammon, R. (2004, December 8-14). Don Perata: The man. *East Bay Express.*

Gifford, B. R. (1985). A modest proposal: Increasing the supply of minority teachers. ED 260-027.

Ginright, S. (2004). *Black in School: Afrocentric Reform, Urban Youth & the Promise of Hip-Hop Culture.* New York: Teachers College Press.

Gitlin, T. (1995, November/December). Rewriting history. *Teacher Magazine.*

Goertz, M. E., & Pitcher, B. (1985, January). The Impact of NTE Use by States on Teacher Selection (RR-85-1), Princeton, NJ: Educational Testing Service.

Goodwin, A. L. (1997). Multicultural stories: Pre-service teachers' conceptions of and responses to issues of diversity. *Urban Education*, 32, 117–145.

Gordon, J. (1997). Teachers of color speak to issues of respect and image. *The Urban Review*, 29, 41–64.

Gordon, J. (2000). *The Color of Teaching.* London: Routledge Falmer.

Gordon, R. (1990). "New Developments in Legal Theory," in D. Kairys, (Ed.) *The Politics of Law*, 2nd ed., New York: Pantheon 413, 424.

Gould, S. J. (June 1, 1996). *The Mismeasure of Man*. New York: W. W. Norton & Company; Rev/Expd edition.

Grillo, T., & Wildman, S. (1991). Obscuring the importance of race: The implication of making comparisons between racism and sexism (or other -isms). *Duke Law Journal*, 1991(2), 397–412.

Guthrie, J. (October 10, 1999). No room at top for women in education. *San Francisco Chronicle*.

Haberman, M. (1986). Alternative teacher certification programs. *Action in Teacher Education*, 8(2), 13–18.

Haberman, M., & Richards, W. H. (1990). Urban teachers who quit: Why they leave and what they do. *Urban Education*, 25(3), 297–303.

Haberman, M. (1991, April 10–12). The Dimensions of Excellence in Programs of Teacher Education. Keynote Address to the First Annual Conference on Alternative Certification, South Padre Island, Texas.

Hamilton, Kendra. (2002, Nov. 21). Crossroads, directions, and a new critical race theory. *Black Issues in Higher Education*, 19(20).

Haney, W., Madaus, G. & Kreitzer, A. (1987). Charms talismanic: Testing teachers for the improvement of American education. *Review of Research in Education*, 14, 169–238.

Haney, W. (2002, May 6). Lake Woebeguaranteed: Misuse of test scores in Massachusetts, Part I. *Education Policy Analysis Archives*, 10(24), 1–27.

Harper, W. & Gammon, R. (2004, December 8–14). Don Perata: The investigation. *East Bay Express*, p. 8.

Hawkins, B. D. (1995, August 10). Kimberly Williams Crenshaw: The making of a critical race theorist. *Black Issues in Higher Education*, 13.

Hayward Unified School District. (1993). Request to the Instructional Material Fund Credit to Purchase Materials Not Adopted by the State Board of Education.

Henig, J. (2000). *The Color of School Reform*. Princeton: Princeton University Press.

Hernandez, B. (1992, June 23). *Oakland Tribune*.

Hodges, S. (2001, October 26). Personal interview.

Hoff, D. J. (2003, Jan 15). Calif. State Senator proposes bailout for Oakland schools. *Education Week*, 22(18), 4.

Hollins, E. (1997, January 3). An open letter to Jessie Jackson. *The Montclarion*, p. 8.

hooks, b. (1994). *Teaching to Transgress: Education as the Practice of Freedom*. New York: Routledge, pp. 1–12.

Hopson, R. H. & Obidah, J.(2002, Summer). When getting tough means getting tougher: Historical and conceptual understandings of juveniles of color sentenced as adults in the United States. *The Journal of Negro Education*, 71(3), 158.

It's about time state takes notice of FCMAT. (2003, August 29). *Oakland Tribune*.

Jackson, I. (1924). Unpublished master's thesis. Berkeley CA: U.C. Berkeley.

Jackson, K. (1996). *America is Me*. New York, NY: Harper Perennial.

Jones, D. L., & Sandidge, R. F. (1997). Recruiting and retaining teachers. *Education and Urban Society*, 29(2).

Katz, A. (2003, January 27). State control of schools has mixed results. *Oakland Tribune*, p. 1.

Katz, A. (2004). See change coming to city schools. *Oakland Tribune*.

Keleher, T., & Libero, D. P. (1999). Creating crisis: How California's teaching policies aggravate racial inequalities in public schools. San Francisco, CA: Applied Research Center.

Kensingon Research Group. (1995, March). Oakland Unified School District and California State University Hayward: A Collaborative Alternative Certification Program Proposal.

Ladson-Billings, G. (1991). Beyond multicultural illiteracy. *Journal of Negro Education*, 60 (2), 147–157.

Ladson-Billings, G. (1992). The liberatory consequences of literacy: A case of culturally relevant instruction for African-American students. *Journal of Negro Education*, 61(3) 378–390.

Ladson-Billings, G., & Tate, W. (1995). A critical race theory of education. *Teachers College Record*, 97, 47–68.

Loewen, J. W. (1996). *Lies My Teacher Told Me: Everything Your American History Textbook Got Wrong*. New York: Touchstone Books.

Luckers, E., Lyters, D., & Fox, M. (2004). Teacher Attrition and Mobility, Results from the Teacher Follow-Up Survey (2001). NCES 2004-301. U.S. Department of Education, National Center for Education Statistics, Washington D.C., U.S. Government Printing Office.

Martinez, E. (1995). Distorting Latino history: The California textbook controversy. In D. Levine, R. Lowe, R. Peterson, & R. Tenorio, *Rethinking Schools*. New York: New Press.

Mayoral takeover of Oakland schools postponed. (1999, Apr. 19). *Education Daily*, 32(73), 7.

McKibbin, M. (2001, Winter). One size does not fit all: Reflections on alternative routes to teacher preparation in California. *Teacher Education Quarterly*, 28 (1), 133.

Mertens, D. (1998). *Research Methods in Education and Psychology*. Thousand Oaks, CA: Sage Publications.

MGO tables Harris bill. (1989, June 27). *The Montclarion*, p. 5.

Minorities, citing bias, sue over test of teachers' skills. (September 24, 1992). *Los Angeles Times*.

Mitchell, B. (1969, June 11). *Oakland Tribune*, p. 1.

Morrow, R. A., & Torres, C. A. (1995). *Social Theory and Education: A Critique of Theories of Social and Cultural Reproduction*. New York: SUNY Press.

Moses, R., and Cobb, C. (2002). *Radical Equations: Civil Rights from Mississippi to the Algebra Project*. Beacon Press.

Nash, G. (1991). *Red, White, and Black: The Peoples of Early North America*. 3rd edition. Englewood Cliffs, NJ: Prentice Hall.

National Center for Education Statistics. (2002). Digest of Education Statistics. Retrieved October 20, 2004 from http://nces.ed.gov/programs/digest/d02/tables/dt224.asp

National Commission on Teaching and America's Future. (2004, May 13). Press Release: At the Fiftieth Anniversary of Brown vs. Board of Education Report Still Finds Millions of Low Income Students and Students of Color Still Concentrated in Separate and Unequal Schools.

Ng, J. C. (2003). Teacher shortages in urban schools: The role of traditional and alternative certification routes in filling the voids. *Education and Urban Society*, 35(4), 380–398.

Oakes, J. (1985). *Keeping Track: How Schools Structure Inequality.* New Haven: Yale University Press.

Oakland Federation of Teachers (1969, July 28) Flier.

Oakland Student Alliance (1970, February) Flier.

Oakland Tribune. (1962, April 22). p. 1.

Oakland Tribune. (September 18, 1968). (Editorial), p. 18.

Oakland Tribune. (1969, October 8). p. 1.

Oakland school board's face-saving decision. (1989, August 28). *San Francisco Chronicle*, p. A4.

Oliver, M., & Shapiro, T. M. (1995). *Black Wealth/White Wealth.* New York: Routledge.

Ouyang, K. (2001, Fall). Contemporary development of Marxist philosophy in China. *Socialism and Democracy*, 15(2), 85.

Partington, G. (1988). The concept of progress in Marxist educational theory. *Comparative Education.* 24(1), 75–87.

Pastor J. Alfred Smith's keynote speech. (1989, November). *Ad Hoc Committee of Parents and Teachers Newsletter*, p. 2.

Payton, B. (2003, August 19). Manipulations seen in school takeover. *Oakland Tribune*, p. A-9.

Perry, T., & Delpit, L. (1998). *The Real Ebonics Debate: Power, Language, and the Education of African-American Children.* New York: Beacon Press.

Persell, C. H. (1977). *Education and Inequality.* New York: The Free Press.

Persell, C. H. (1979). *Education and Inequality.* New York: The Free Press.

Phillips, S. (1968, Dec. 3). Responses to Demands Presented by Associated Students Union of Oakland. Oakland Public Schools Office of the Superintendent

Put the heat on school leaders. (1989, July 20). *The Tribune*, p. A-16.

Rafsky, R. (1970, March 1). Interview with Marcus Foster. Philadelphia Bulletin.

Ravitch, D. (2000). *Left Back: A Century of Battles Over School Reform.* New York: Touchstone.

Reading between the lines. (2002, Jan 28). *The Nation.*

Rehberg, R. (1978). *Class and Merit in the American High School.* London: Longman.

Report on the final evaluation of the city-state partnership (2001). Presented to the New Baltimore City Board of Commissioners and the Maryland State Department of Education. Rockville, Maryland: Westat.

Rhomberg, C. (1998, Winter). White nativism and urban politics: The 1920s and the Ku Klux Klan in Oakland, California. *Journal of American Ethnic History*, 17(2), 39.

Sack, J. (2002, May 1). Michigan may intervene in Inkster-Edison standoff. *Education Week*, p.1.

Schaerer, J. W. (1996). Perceived Supply and Demand of Minority Teachers and Administrators in the Southwest United States. Research report prepared under the sponsorship of Arkansas State University, Eastern Kentucky University and Georgia University, Athens (ERIC Document Reproduction Service No. ED 405 292).

Scheiffer, J. (2000). Highlights of the Commission. Counselors and Analysts of California. Retrieved February 20, 2004 from www.teamccac.org/highlights/72000.html

Self, R. O. (2004). *American Babylon: Race and the Struggle for Postwar Oakland.* Princeton, NJ: Princeton University Press.

Shaw, C. (1996). The big picture: An inquiry into the motivations of African-American teacher education students to be or not to be teachers. *American Educational Researcher*, 33 (2), 327–354.

Shorr, J. (1997, August 18). Training ground for teachers. *Oakland Tribune.*

Sinclair, U. (1924). *The Goslings.* Pasadena, California.

Sleeter, C., & Grant, C. A. (1991). *Making Choices for Multicultural Education: Five Approaches for Race, Class, and Gender*, 2nd ed. New York: Macmillan.

Sleeter, C. (1996). *Multicultural Education As Social Activism.* New York: SUNY Press.

Smith, T. M., Rogers, G.T., Alsalam, N., Perie, M., Mahoney, R. P. & Martin, V. (1994). The condition of education. Washington, DC. National Center for Education Statistics, U.S. Department of Education ED 371 491.

Snapp, M. (1999, December 31). A century of famous faces in Oakland. *The Montclarion*, p. 8.

Snyder, T. D., & Hoffman, C. M. (1994). Digest of Education Statistics, 1994, Washington, DC. National Center for Education Statistics, U.S. Department of Education ED 377 253.

Solorzano, D. G., & Ornela, A. (2004, Feb/Mar). A critical race analysis of Latina/o and African American advanced placement enrollment in public high schools. *The High School Journal.* 87(3), 15.

Southern Regional Education Board (SREB). (2003). Spinning Our Wheels. Atlanta. Retrieved November 5, 2004 from http://www.sreb.org/main/publications/pubs/Spinning_Wheels.pdf

Staples, B. (1997, January 24). The last train from Oakland. *New York Times,* p. 30.

Stoskopf, A. (2002, Winter). Echoes of a forgotten past: Eugenics, testing, and education reform. *The Educational Forum,* 66(2), 126.

Superintendents Bulletin (1925, October). Oakland Public Schools.

Teach for America. (2004). How It Works. Retrieved November 1, 2004 from http://www.teachforamerica.com/paid.html

Terman, L. (1916). *The Measurement of Intelligence.* Boston: Houghton Mifflin

Thompson, C. (2004, December 8–14). Don Perata: The machine. *East Bay Express.*

Trueba, E. (1998) "Critical Ethnography and a Vygotskian Pedagogy of Hope: The Case of Mexican Immigrant Children." *In Latinos Unidos: From Cultural Diversity to the Politics of Solidarity* (Lanham: Rowman and Littlefield Publishers, Inc.)

Tyack, D. (1974). *The One Best System.* Cambridge, MA: Harvard University Press.

U.S. Department of Education. (1999). National Center for Education Statistics, Common Core of Data survey unpublished data. Retrieved February 22, 2004 from http://nces.ed.gov/surveys/ruraled/data/Race_Ethnicity.asp

U.S. Department of Education. (2000). National Center for Education Statistics. Retrieved February 22, 2004 from http://nces.ed.gov/edstats/index.asp

Viadero, D. (1991, February 20). Social-studies texts face renewed challenge in L.A. vote. *Education Week.*

Wallis, V. (1998).The Communist manifesto and capitalist hegemony after 150 years. *Socialism and Democracy.* 12(1-2), 7.

Wattenberg, B. (1995, November 23) (Interview) A Conversation with Todd Gitlin (Transcript). Think Tank: PBS Television Network. Retrieved January 20, 2005 from www.pbs.org/thinktank/transcript235.html

Waugh, D. (1990, Aug. 10) History textbook feud splits sides on racial lines. *The Examiner.* P. A1

Waugh, D. (1992, May 17). *The Examiner.* B1.

What Matters Most: Teaching For America's Future. (1996, September). Report of the National Commission on Teaching and America's Future.

Wilder, R. (1999, August 27). Ebonics is working: Three years later. *AfroAmerican Red Star,* p. A1.

Williams, R. L. (1997). The Ebonics controversy. *Journal of Black Psychology,* 23(3), 208–214.

Willie, C. V. (1991). The social and historical context: A case study of philanthropic assistance. In C. V. Willie, A. M. Garibaldi, & W. L. Reed. *The Education of African Americans.* New York: Auburn House.

Wilson, A. J. (1984). *Knowledge for Teachers; The National Teacher Examination Program, 1940 to 1970.* Unpublished doctoral dissertation, University of Wisconsin. (University Microfilms International No. 84-14265).

Witty, E. (1982). Prospects for Black teachers: Preparation, certification, employment. Washington, DC. ERIC Clearinghouse on Teacher Education ED 213 659.

Yeo, F. (1997). Teacher preparation and inner-city schools: Sustaining educational failure. *The Urban Review,* 29(2), 127–143.

Zane, M. (1970, April 7). New Oakland school chief tells goal. *San Francisco Chronicle,* p. 1.

Index

Studies in the Postmodern Theory of Education

General Editors
Joe L. Kincheloe & Shirley R. Steinberg

Counterpoints publishes the most compelling and imaginative books being written in education today. Grounded on the theoretical advances in criticalism, feminism, and postmodernism in the last two decades of the twentieth century, Counterpoints engages the meaning of these innovations in various forms of educational expression. Committed to the proposition that theoretical literature should be accessible to a variety of audiences, the series insists that its authors avoid esoteric and jargonistic languages that transform educational scholarship into an elite discourse for the initiated. Scholarly work matters only to the degree it affects consciousness and practice at multiple sites. Counterpoints' editorial policy is based on these principles and the ability of scholars to break new ground, to open new conversations, to go where educators have never gone before.

For additional information about this series or for the submission of manuscripts, please contact:

Joe L. Kincheloe & Shirley R. Steinberg
c/o Peter Lang Publishing, Inc.
29 Broadway, 18th floor
New York, New York 10006

To order other books in this series, please contact our Customer Service Department:

(800) 770-LANG (within the U.S.)
(212) 647-7706 (outside the U.S.)
(212) 647-7707 FAX

Or browse online by series:
www.peterlang.com